ALL *the* HOPE *in the* BIBLE

ORDINARY FOLKS DOING EXTRAORDINARY THINGS

JEAN BACON WHITE

WESTBOW°
PRESS
A DIVISION OF THOMAS NELSON
& ZONDERVAN

NIV Study Bible, Zondervan, 1984
The New Unger's Bible dictionary, Moody press, 1977
Strongest, NIV, Exhaustive Concordance, Zondervan 1999
Israel Pocket library, History Until 1880, Keter books, Jerusalem, Israel 1973
Chronological and Background Charts of the Old Testament, Revised and Expanded Edition, John H. Walton, Zondervan 1994
Things to Come, J. Dwight Pentecost, Zondervan 1958

WestBow Press books may be ordered through booksellers or by contacting:

WestBow Press
A Division of Thomas Nelson & Zondervan
1663 Liberty Drive
Bloomington, IN 47403
www.westbowpress.com
1 (866) 928-1240

ISBN: 978-1-4908-7252-0 (sc)
ISBN: 978-1-4908-7254-4 (hc)
ISBN: 978-1-4908-7253-7 (e)

Library of Congress Control Number: 2015903964

Print information available on the last page.

WestBow Press rev. date: 05/07/2015

Dedication

To you the reader

May the God of hope fill you

With all joy and peace

As you trust in Him,

So that you may overflow with hope,

By the power of the Holy Spirit

Romans 15:13

Contents

An introduction to the New Testament

PREFACE

Our lives are moved by cause and effect. The first cause was God and the Bible is his story; our history from beginning to end. He was the creator of the universe and all creation, including mankind. They have always been under his care and control.

His power, glory and love and compassion have been revealed to us by witnesses in his book.

JOEL 3:16 …THE Lord will be a refuge for his people.

Romans 15:13 May the God of hope fill you with all joy and peace as you trust in him, so that you may overflow with hope, by the power of the Holy Spirit.

Psalm 139:1-4 O Lord you have searched me and know me…Before a word is on my tongue, you know it completely, O Lord. (He is all knowing)

Isaiah 40:28 …The Lord is the everlasting God, the creator of the ends of the earth…his understanding no one can fathom.

Romans 11:33 O, the depths of the riches of the wisdom and knowledge of God.

We cannot understand his wisdom, but we can trust in it. He always provides a way of escape from the messes we get ourselves into. Repentance and prayer change everything.

He is everywhere present! No boundaries contain him, no time or space restrict him.

Psalm 139:7... Where can I go from your spirit? Where can I flee from your presence? (He is everywhere present)

Acts 17:27-28 A quake opened the prison doors.

God is always available to those who love him, never missing.

He is all powerful.

Genesis 18:14... Is anything too powerful for the lord...?

Next year Sarah will have a child even though it is not possible at her age!

2 Chronicles 20:6...You rule over all the kingdoms of the nations. Power and might are in your hands and no one can withstand you.

John 32:17 ...nothing is too hard for you.

Hebrews 6:18 ... We who have fled to take hold of the hope offered to us, may be greatly encouraged. We have this hope as an anchor for the soul, firm and secure....

God's promises should rule, not our feelings or our circumstances. His promises are always yea and amen.

Introduction to the Old Testament

The first five books were written by Moses and dictated by God. It is the most ancient of our ancient history.

Moses was a Jewish baby who escaped the sword of a king who sought to slaughter all the Jew's baby boys and missed him, because his mother put him in a basket in the river that went by the king's palace, where his childless daughter bathed. She found him and raised him as her own, with his real mother as his nursemaid. He was part of both worlds and had all the privileges and education of a prince of Egypt, preparing him for the mission which God had for him.

The books that follow these show us that God was always in charge of their destiny. Even in the worst of times. God always had a remnant of his chosen people to continue his fight against evil and produce leaders to further his cause. No matter how much they were persecuted by God's enemies, he always raised up a leader to carry his message of love and hope for the human race and their final liberation, from the forces of evil that tormented them. The Bible is the story of reconciliation between God and man, from Genesis to Revelation, and hope is the thread that holds it all together.

God commanded Moses to write on a scroll. (Exodus 17:14)

PART 1

The beginning of HOPE

GENESIS: IN THE BEGINNING, GOD

The first chapter of the book of Genesis gives us the story of creation; A practical explanation of how the universe came to be, in a process that is scientifically correct. You can follow the progression of days in perfect order to produce a world in which every living creature may live and thrive in harmony with its environment. A planet where everything needed to support human life; in just the right amounts and combinations of elements necessary for our existence and sustenance; a home for us. As far as we know, there is none other like it.

When all was ready, God created man on the sixth day. Male and female he created them and put them in a perfect garden, with perfect bodies in a perfect environment, where they could live forever, with God as their father walking with them in the cool of the evening. There was only one tree that they could not touch on pain of death. It was the tree that stood in the center of the garden. It was exquisite, with tantalizing fruit and a beautiful creature who occupied the branches and spoke to them, in a voice of authority, telling them that the fruit would make them like God. Having been given free will to choose, Eve took a bite and shared it with her husband who stood mesmerized beside her. God's enemy, had won the first round. Sin had entered their world and there was not to be a happily ever after.

Their bodies became like ours and they were exiled to make their way by the sweat of their brows, in a world full of hardship and woe. They had children and the first family became the first dysfunctional family. A son Cain, killed his brother Able in a jealous rage. God gave them another son to take his place. His name was Seth and it was his line that came back to God. They also had other sons and daughters. (Genesis 5:4)

Seth also had a son, and he named him Enosh. At that time men began to call on the name of the Lord. (Genesis 4:26.)

Many generations later came Enoch. He walked with God and then he was no more, because God took him away. He lived here 365 years and his son Methuselah lived to be 969 years old, the oldest man in the Bible.

His son Lamech was the father of Noah who was 500 years old when he became the father of Shem, Ham and Japheth. (5:32)

The Godly and ungodly had intermarried until all godliness had disappeared except for the family of Noah, God's hope for the world. It was time for a new beginning. God made him a preacher of righteousness for 120 years, laboring to bring his countrymen back to God. (Gen. 6:1-9; 1Peter 3:20; 2 Peter 2:5).

Nobody paid attention, so God's judgment would fall upon them. Noah was given instructions to build an ark to house him and his family and every kind of creature, to save them from the flood that would destroy the rest. The people laughed and scorned him. It did not rain there, and there were no waterways to float an ark. They walked by sight and human reasoning, not realizing that nothing is impossible with God!

There was no hope for the scoffers who had refused the master of the universe. Their creator had done everything possible to get their attention and now the Ark was ready and God shut the door. For forty days and 40 nights the rains came and the ark landed on the mountains of Ararat. In time the waters receded and man was again able to live on the earth once more. God sent a rainbow to signify his promise to never again destroy the world with water. The family of Noah, three sons and their wives, would once again follow God's will to populate the world, and his sons were founders of the nations.

PART 2

The rise of nations

Prehistory (history begins with the first exactly dated year 4241 BC)

They say that Neanderthals roamed the earth in 45,000 BC

Settlements of cultures with technologies and social organization existed in 10,000 BC in the near east.

Rise of urbanism: Cain went into exile in Genesis 4:16 and built a city named for his son Enoch.

Enoch's son Irad had Mahujael who had Methushael (man of God) who had Lamech, the first polygamist and first poet and arrogant purveyor of cruelty.

His sons: Jabel, father of those who live in tents and have livestock (nomads)

Jubal, father of those who play the lyre and pipe

Tubal Cain, forger of all instruments of bronze and iron

From Cain we have 6 generations of cultural development and civilization

Seth at 105 had Enosh and lived 807 years more and had more children.

Enosh had Kenan at age ninety and lived 815 more years and had more children.

"Then men began to call on the name of the Lord."

Kenan had Mahalalel, lived 140 years more and had more children.

Mahalelel (praise of God) had Jared at 65 and lived 830 years more and had more children.

Jared at 162 had Enoch, lived 800 more years and had more children.

Enoch at 65 had Methusaleh, lived 300 years more and had more children. "Enoch walked with God and was taken" He did not die. He appears again in the New Testament.

Methuselah (man of the dart) at 187 had Lamech and lived 782 years more and had more children.

Lamech had Noah at 182, lived 595 years more and had more children. "Out of the ground, which the Lord has cursed, this one shall bring us relief from our work and from the toil of our hands."

Noah after 500 years and had Ham, Shem, and Japheth. After this came the flood. Noah was 600 at the beginning of the flood and Shem was 98 at the end.

RISE OF NATIONS AFTER THE FLOOD

An unknown span of years passed between the time of the flood and the dispersion of the families of Noah's sons.

Noah had planted a vineyard and harvested grapes mature enough for the making of wine (Genesis 9:20-21)

Ham had become the father of Canaan in verse 22 and disgraced himself in 22-23 and this son was cursed for his father's sin 25-27. Noah's sons had already received the blessing and could not be cursed. Noah saw the potential in Canaan that was in his father. The Canaanites are known for their grossly immoral behavior.

Ham, was the youngest son of Noah: Imperial power began in Babel, Erech, Accad, and Calneh (Gen.10:10), among the earliest capitals of the civilized world, located in the area which is the entire alluvial plain of Babylon between the Tigris and Euphrates rivers.

To the north was Accad, with the cities of Babel and Accad. In the south was Sumar, with the cities of Erech, Ancient Uruk and modern Warka

HAM'S DESCENDANTS

Cush: father of Seba, Havilah, Sabta, Raamah, Sabteca and Nimrod. (First mentioned king).

Seba was the father of the Sabeans who made a southward migration about 1000 BC. Priest kings were known from the ninth century to the fifth. In 950 BC the queen of Seba traveled 1200 miles to the north to visit Solomon.

Havilah (Gen. 2:8) The Pishon river runs all the way through the whole land of Havilah, a land of gold, onyx, and bdellium and aromatic gum, a place north of Seba, where nomadic tribes of Ishmael dwelled (1 Samuel 15:7). Their descendants were the Assyrians.

Raamah: Known as traders in Ezekiel 27:22 Seba: inscriptions call it a place in SW Arabia referred to as Regma in LXX and the Vulgate.

Sons of Raamah are Sheba and Dedan on the shores of the Persian Gulf.

Nimrod First King and a rebel: Evil Babylonian system and Sumerian dynasty of Kish which had 23 kings in a military state by force.

He was the opposite of what God wanted kings to be. He was a mighty hunter. The hunter kills his victims to satisfy himself, but the shepherd king does what is best for his subjects. (2 Samuel 5:2; 7:7; Revelation 2:27) All his subjects were: Babel, Erech, Accad, and Calneh (10:10) in the land of Shinar. (So. Mesopotamia)

Ham's son Mizraim (Gen. 10:6; 13-14; 1 Chronicles 1:8, and11-12) Egypt. Nations: Lud, Anam, Lehab, Naphtah, Pathrus, Casluh and Caphtor, Lud-Lydians, (Gen.10:13; I Chronicles 1:11-17; Isaiah 66:19 (Ezekiel 27:10; 30:5) Ludim, Lydians (Eze. 30:5; Jeremiah 46:9.)

Lydia 700 BC: wealthy and powerful minters of gold and silver money. The kingdom ended with King Croesus in 546 BC. They became a part of Pergamum which became a part of the Roman province of Asia in 133 BC. In Revelation, cities of Thyatira, Sardis and Philadelphia. (2:18-3:13).

Anam: an unknown Egyptian tribe.

Lehab: Midianite stock, Libyans: fair haired, blue eyed in Egyptian army in 19th and 20th dynasties. Shishak in 22nd dynasty is first pharaoh mentioned In the Bible (945-924 BC) His gold masked body was found in the temple at Karnak (ancient Thebes). He plundered Solomon's temple and fought against Palestine. There is a Stele at Megiddo.

Naphtuh in Egypt or west of it.

Pathrus-upper Egypt (southland) Thebais in classic geography and Paturissu in cuneiform texts.

Casluh-Philistines between Pathrus and Chaphtor.

Chaphtor-Crete (Deuteronomy 2:23) migrant from Egypt-part of sea peoples, finally settling in Canaan.

Put (Phut)-Coast of Somaliland, connected to Egypt (soldiers).

Canaan-Egyptian name for all of western Syria-arts and sciences, walled cities, ceramic arts, music, musical instruments and architecture; Palestine and Phoenicia. Solomon's temple artisans and architects, Hiram of Tyre (1 Kings 7:13-51) fortresses, palaces, temples etc. Ivory, gold, and alabaster from Megiddo.-Excavated cities=Jerico, Bethal, Libnuh, Debir, Megiddo, Beth Shean, Beth Shemish, Byblos, Ras Shamra and Geza. There were fertility cults, lewd immoral gods, prostitute goddesses, serpents, doves and bulls. The head God was El and his son was Baal.

The sons of Canaan.

Sidon=Lebanon-Tyre, seafarers, oldest capital of Phoenicia (Gen. 10:15). The Amarna letters in 1400 called them Sidonians from the 11th to 18th centuries. From them we have: Jezebel, philosophy, astronomy, and Baal worship. They were the Hittites of Asia Minor, a great power at the time of the first dynasty of Babylon and third most influential ancients of the mid- east. They had horses and Iron and the great cities of Tarsus, Iconium, and Lystra.

Jebusities, Jerusalem (Jebus). They were mountaineers of the hill country, warlike, on the border between Judah and Benjamin.

Amorites-westerner-tall ones (Palestine, Phoenicia, (Amarna). It was later called Amurru, Syria, Palestine Home of Hammurabi and his code of law.

GIRGASHITES WEST OF THE JORDAN

Hivites (Tent village) Gen.34:2-31: peaceful, democratic, diplomats, traders and farmers. They were located in the land of Mizpeh, a district of Gilead which is from the Sea of Galilee to the Dead Sea.

Arkites in present day Arka about 30 miles north of Sidon at the foot of Lebanon, conquered by Thutmose III in the 15th century BC and by Assyria in 738 BC.

Sinites-In Targums of Onkelos, use Orthosia, a maritime town south east of Tripois, important because it controlled the only road between Phoenicia and the maritime parts of Syria.

Arvadite-the Island of Aradus (Arvad) off the coast of Syria. They became involved in Phoenician affairs, especially after Tyre and Sidon fell to Greco-Syrian kings.

Zemarites,-probably Mt. Zemaraim

Hamathites-In Joshua 19:35 it's a fortified city. In Josephus it is Emmaus.

The sons of Shem

Aram: from the Lebanon Mountains, to beyond the Euphrates river and from the Taurus range to Damascus and northern Palestine on the south.

Contact with Hebrews: (Gen. 28:5) as Padam Aram and (Gen 31:47) with the patriarchs. He was maternal ancestor of Jacob's children (Deuteronomy 26:5).

While Israel wandered and while judges ruled, they were multiplying and extending in every direction, particularly southward

In the time of Saul, they began to clash with Israel and became prominent in the Old Testament.

Many great kings and kingdoms flourished until conquered by David who added them to his kingdom, an empire for Solomon.

The Aramaic language (once called Chaldee because it was spoken by some Chaldeans. (Daniel 2:4-7, 28; Ezra 4;8-6:18; 7:12-26; Jeramiah 10:11) written in the Aramaic language of the Persian period in SW Asia for trade and business from Armana 500-400BC, (Elephantine in upper Egypt).

The Greeks called Aramaic-Syriac, spoken at Edessa, which became the language of Christian churches in Syria and Mesopotamia.

Arphachshad was the first post flood patriarch as father of Shelah, born two years after the flood.

They occupied the mountain country of the upper Zab River NNE of Nineveh.

Assur had an Assyria dominated empire from the 9th to the 7th century BC, until it was taken over by the neo Babylonian empire.

Elam was bounded on the north, by Assyria and Media and on the south by the Persian Gulf (Gen. 14:11) in Abraham's era. They were conquered by Persians (Ezekiel 32:24; Ezra 4:9).

Shem's territory was a straight line from the Mediterranean Sea to the Indian Ocean, intersecting lands of Ham and Japheth.

Joktan, grandson of Shem, located on the Arabian Peninsula.

Japheth had seven sons who were the Aryan nations of Europe: Greece, Italy, Germany, France, Scandinavia, England, Scotland, and Ireland.

PART 3

Abraham, a Covenant with God

God's man for his time, from paganism to God; father of many nations and claimed by Christians, Jews and Muslims.

Abraham was from the line of Shem and lived in Ur of the Chaldees, a pagan land that did not know the one true God, but worshiped the moon God Sin.

In Genesis 12, God spoke to him, telling him to leave his country and his father's house and go to a place that God would show him.

"I will make you into a great nation and I will bless you. I will make your name great and you will be a blessing. I will bless those who bless you, and whoever curses you, I will curse, and all the people on earth will be blessed through you."

He listened carefully to all that God told him, and obeyed, taking his wife and his fatherless nephew lot and all his household and their possessions and set out on an unknown path to an unknown place and a future directed by God alone for the rest of his life. Is it any wonder that he is listed in the hall of fame of the faithful in Hebrews chapter 11? He probably took his nephew along, because he was old and childless and had no heir.

Abraham journeyed to Canaan and there God spoke to him again and told him, that one day his descendants would own this land. Then, he went to Egypt and back again. He had a falling out with lot, because their flocks were too many for the land they occupied. Abraham gave him a choice of two acceptable sections and he chose the plain of the Jordan. Abraham stayed where he was.

It was here that God promised a son by his wife Sarah and posterity as the sand is, by the sea, or the stars in the sky and the Bible reveals that it happened Just as God promised.

Lot was stripped of his wealth by a nearby king and Abraham went after him and brought him and everything else back with him. It was at that time that he met Melchizedek, priest of the Most High God, and gave him a tithe of the spoils of his victory over the wicked king.

God made a covenant with Abraham, (a contract), a covenant of land.

God said, "Know for certain that your descendants will be strangers in a country not their own, and they will be enslaved and mistreated four hundred years. But, I will punish the nation they serve as slaves and afterward they will come out with great possessions. You, however will go to your fathers in peace and be buried at a good old age." He knew they would come back and possess the land. (Genesis 15)

Ten years later 75 year old Sarah, Abraham's wife, decided to follow the custom of her day for childless wives, to select a surrogate mother for her child, and she sent her husband to her maid servant Hagar to father a child for her, and Ishmael was conceived.

Thirteen years after this, God gave a covenant sign for all the men to be circumcised. Starting with Abraham and his family and all the others of his household, when Abraham was 99 years old. (17-21) He was also told that in one year, his wife would bear the promised son.

When Isaac was born, both Hagar and Ishmael were jealous and tension grew between the two mothers to such an extreme that God told Abraham to send them away and that he would bless Ishmael; with twelve nations. (The Arab nations of today) He also said that there would always be enmity between the two boys. (Jews and Muslims even now)

Abraham's greatest test of his faith came when God told him to go up on the mountain and take Isaac as a sacrifice, when the boy was 25 years old. (Josephus Ant. 1.13.2). He knew God did not want human sacrifice and that God's promise to make his descendants as many as the sand of the seashore and the stars in the sky depended on Isaac. He also knew that God could raise the dead. He continued to walk by faith and when the boy asked, "Where is the sheep." He replied, "God will provide." And as Abraham raised his knife, a sheep was there in the thicket just in time. He had passed the test.

Sarah died at 127, and it was time for Isaac to marry. His father sent a servant back to Haran and God gave him a sign that he should choose Rebekah, the daughter of Abraham's brother, Nahor.

Abraham married a second wife named Keturah, and she bore him six sons and they were settled in the east so they would not interfere with Isaac.

The Promised Land, was a hope for Abraham and he even lived in it for a time, but it was meant for future generations. His nephew Lot chose to live in Sodom and lived to regret it. It was such an evil city that God destroyed it, after warning lot and his family to leave and never look back. His wife did and was turned into a pillar of salt.

In times of trouble God provides a way of escape for those who know and trust him

Abraham met God's enemies, famine, domestic problems, and all means of trouble, but never lost his faith. God's promises bring hope in the midst of trials and tribulations. Faith in God means surrender to his will, knowing he will never leave us or forsake us, even when hope seems futile and depression tells us to turn away.

Abraham's story is an example of how a man's trust in God's promises always brings them to pass.

Isaac received the covenant blessing when his father died and when he had twin sons, Esau and Jacob, it was passed on to Jacob. For as the Lord said at their birth, that the older would serve the younger. It was by Jacob's 12 sons that the future promise would be fulfilled, as the twelve tribes became the children of Israel, the people of God who would inhabit the Promised Land.

PART 4

Jacob, Becomes Israel

Twelve tribes and their impact on the history of hope

Jacob is now the bearer of the covenant which God bestowed on his father and grandfather. A promised land still loomed in the future, a gift from God to them, a promise to Abraham, Isaac and Jacob, a place of rest from wandering the earth for so many years.

Jacob has returned from many years in the land of his uncle Laban with great wealth and twelve sons, two wives and concubines. He went there to marry Rachel, whom he loved, and his uncle tricked him into marrying her older sister first and then be in servitude for seven years before he could have the one he wanted The wives vied for his affection by providing as many sons as possible and even used their maids to outdo one another in providing them.

By Leah the first wife he had six sons: Reuben, Simeon, Issachar, Zebulun, Levi, and Judah. Reuben lost favor with his father when he went in and slept with one of his concubines, Bilhah. But he saved the life of his brother Joseph when the others would have killed him out of jealousy, because he was their dad's favorite, having been born to his favorite wife, Rachel. They sold him into slavery instead.

God had a plan for Joseph that would make the difference between life and death for his family. He was sold to a rich man named Potiphar and given command over his household. When the man's wife wanted to have an affair with him, he ran away from her. To get even, she convinced her husband that he had attacked her and Joseph was put in prison. It was all part of God's plan. He was put in charge of all the prisoners and interpreted dreams and they came true. One of these was for the king's cupbearer, who was freed from prison and later when the king had dreams, which his magicians could not interpret, he remembered Joseph. Joseph was able to explain his dreams and the king gave him charge over his kingdom only second to him.

It was Joseph who knew the famine was coming and had made great preparations for the storage of grain in huge amounts, so no one in Egypt would go hungry. There was even enough to help people from outside to share.

Reuben went into Egypt for food in time of the famine with brothers, but dad kept the youngest, Benjamin, at home, being the only son of his beloved Rachel who had died at his birth. He still mourned the loss of Joseph. It was a shock to the brothers to have to deal with Joseph, in order to get food for the family. The brothers were afraid he would harm them for what they had done, but he was happy to have news of his father and brother and tricked them into bringing them to Egypt and all was well.

At the exodus, the tribe of Rueben had grown to 46,500 men over 20 and fit for military service.

Simeon was just and devout and promised by God, that he would see the Messiah before he died and he did. (Luke 2:25-35)

Levi and his brother Simeon Plotted to get even when their sister Dinah was raped by Shechem. (Gen.34) He had also taken part in selling Joseph to the Ishmaelites. His father, on his deathbed, reminded him of his crime

Levi was father of the tribe who became the Levites, who were keepers of the sanctuary under the authority of the priests.

Judah was the one who told his brothers to sell Joseph, to save his life. He married a daughter of a Canaanite and had three sons. He refused to honor his daughter- in- law Tamar who had been widowed by two of his sons and left childless. Under law he was supposed to give her the other son, who was too young, or take her as wife himself. When he refused, she posed as a temple prostitute and tricked him into giving her twin sons.

Judah became leader over his brothers and finally led the family to live in the land of Goshen, as Joseph, the brother who had been sold into slavery, now became their benefactor under Pharaoh.

By the first census, his three sons had grown families that totaled 74,600 as the largest tribe.

Caleb, the faithful man who with Joshua went into the Promised Land, was one of his descendants. His banner was green with the symbol of a lion.

Dan was the fifth son of Jacob, by Bilhah, Rachel's maid. (Gen. 30:6). At the exodus, the tribe had 62,700 warriors. Samson was a Danite. (Judges 13:2) Oholiab (Ex. 31:6) was an expert in working with metals, in charge of preparing objects for the tabernacle.

Naphtali, second son by Bilhah, brother to Dan, when Israel went down to Egypt had 4 sons. At the first census, the tribe numbered

53,400. Their one true hero was Barak of Kadesh. They were the first tribe to be taken by the Assyrians.

Gad was the first son by Zilpah, Leah's maid. At the time they went down into Egypt, they included seven sons. At the first Census Gad had 45,650 adult males following the banner of Reuben. They were a warrior tribe contributing to the conquest of Canaan. They succeeded to accomplish a great victory over Ishmael's descendants. Many of the Gadite leaders served under King David. Finally they too were taken by the Assyrians.

Asher had four sons and one daughter. When they left Egypt, they were 41,500 in the tribe and at the second census they had grown to 53,400. Being neighbor to the Phoenicians, they became weak and of little worth. When David ruled, their name had disappeared from the record.

Simeon and Asher, west of the Jordan gave no Judges or heroes. The one exception is Anna a daughter of the tribe of Asher, a Godly prophetess who held the baby Jesus and proclaimed him Messiah.

Issachar was the fifth son of Leah. Going down to Egypt, he had 3 sons and 57,400 fighting men and at the second census had 64,300. He paid tribute to the raiding tribes who were after their abundant crops.

Zebulun was the sixth and last son of Leah. Going down to Egypt he had 3 sons with 57,400. Nazareth and Cana were in its territory.

Joseph, first born son of Rachel, and his father's favorite, caused jealousy among his many brothers. He had dreams and visions concerning them and their future relationship. They first plotted to kill him but sold him into slavery instead. When famine came, he was in charge of pharaoh's food supplies and saved their lives

Benjamin, was the youngest, and final child of Rachel, which cost her life at birth. Going down to Egypt it was 35,400 and by the next census was 45,600. They assisted the judge, Deborah, and were almost wiped out. Their most prominent member was King Saul, the first king of the Jews. They became allied with Judah and Jerusalem was in their district.

As you can see, the descendants of Abraham are growing in great numbers and this is just from one grandson and he had eight sons and we know that God had promised Ishmael twelve nations.

PART 5

Moses, and the Exodus

He was born in Egypt in the time of slavery after Joseph had died. His parents were of the tribe of Levi, and he was a son of Amram and Jochabed, with siblings, Aaron and Miriam. According to Josephus, his birth was foretold to pharaoh by his magicians and to his father by a dream. The decree to slay all Jewish baby boys was still in force. (Exodus 1:10-16). His mother put him in a basket in the Nile where Pharaoh's childless daughter would find him and God helped her become his nursemaid.

God had planned the life of Moses to prepare him for the future of his people Israel, to free them from 400 years in Egypt and lead them to the Promised Land. They were in bondage, with no hope.

He grew up as a prince of Egypt, but never became Egyptian. His heart was always for God's people.

He killed an Egyptian who was abusing a Jewish slave, and had to flee to the desert. He was called by God from a burning bush which was not consumed, as he tended sheep in Midian, to be the deliverer of his people. But, Moses had a speech impediment and God allowed him to bring his brother Aaron to speak for him to pharaoh.

He was given special powers to make the ruler listen to him and let his people go, but it was no use. The angry man refused to lose his slaves. God sent 10 plagues to change his mind. The first plague was turning all the water into blood. The second was a plague of frogs. The third was gnats. The forth was flies. The fifth was against the livestock. The sixth was boils. The seventh was hail. The eighth was locusts that ate everything in sight. The ninth was total darkness. Each of these phenomena was a horror of extremes, but this stony hearted man had no pity on his people and refused to give any credence to Moses' God until the tenth plague took the firstborn of every house except for the Jews, whom God exempted from all the plagues. The people gave them all kinds of valuables to get them to go away and pharaoh sent them on their way, but the ruler was not finished with them. He sent his army after them and they caught up with them at the Red Sea and God performed another miracle. He opened a road through the water for them to pass through on dry ground and it rolled back over the Egyptian army and kept them safe.

Moses had been in Egypt for forty years and in Midian for forty years and was 80 years old when he led the children of Israel out of 400 years of bondage. Now they would spend 40 years wandering in the wilderness because when they got to the Promised Land, the ones who went to spy it out were afraid to go in because of the fierce looking men and walled cities. Only Joshua and Caleb were willing to obey God and Go take it for their own. God would not let them have it until all the generations of the naysayers were gone.

During the wanderings God directed them with a cloud by day and fire by night. The tribes were regimented by Moses, each in its place and leadership appointed, and they became an army of the Lord able to keep themselves safe and where God wanted them to be at all times.

A tabernacle was portable as a place of worship. It was made by skilled craftsman according to God's directions. It was an elaborate place for the presence of God to meet with man and housed the Ark of the Covenant at its center. It contained the tablets of stone on which were written The Ten Commandments and on the top of it were two Cherubim made of pure gold and it was lined and covered in pure gold. There were rings which held the poles by which it was carried because to touch it meant certain death. (Exodus 25-28 and 35-40)

Manna was provided for food each day and when people got out of line God punished them. During this time, Moses went up on the mountain and met with God and brought back the Ten Commandments. His face shown so that others could not look at him when he returned. At one point they were short on water and God told Moses to speak to the rock and water would come out to show that God's power was still watching over them, but Moses got angry and pounded on the stone and he got the credit. This fault kept him from entering the Promised Land.

The book of the law; Deuteronomy, is Moses legacy, a farewell to his people, laying out their history, repeating all the commands they have been given and the lessons they have learned in his care. They are all commanded to remember to pass on to their children all that has happened to them in their wanderings with God. They must know all; the good, the bad, and the ugly and learn from it. The Ten Commandments appear in chapter 5:6-21 with explanations of how to use them in daily life. In simple form they say:

You shall have no other Gods before me. You shall not make for yourself any carved image. You shall not take the name of your God in vain. Observe the Sabbath to keep it holy. Honor your father and mother. You shall not murder. You shall not commit adultery. You shall not steal. You shall not bear false witness against your neighbor. You shall not covet.

There is a covenant renewal, demanding absolute allegiance, and confession. There are curses and blessings. (Chapters 27-30) God is both justified and the justifier. No one can reject his law without consequences, Forgiveness only comes to those mournfully repentant. The cursed are only those who are not. It's a matter of the heart. Yield and be saved. There is no hope otherwise. The law reveals our need for God, for no man can keep it all. We have no righteousness except in him.

When the time of penance was done God took Moses up Mount Nebo and allowed him to see the land that had been promised to Abraham, Isaac and Jacob and it was time to pass the people's care into the hands of Joshua, God's faithful servant through all the good and all the bad times.

God's servant, Moses died and was buried and no one has ever found his grave.

PART 6

Joshua

He was leader, warrior, and statesman. Joshua was faithful against all odds. When all the spies went to check out the Promised Land, he and Caleb were the only ones ready to obey the command of God to go in and possess the land. The representatives of the other tribes were afraid of the fortified cities and huge men. The consequences were a harsh forty years of wandering in the wilderness.

Joshua was of the tribe of Ephraim, a son of Joseph, and along with Caleb, of the tribe of Judah, were the only survivors of that generation. Now their hope in the Lord's promise was about to be fulfilled.

He had been Moses' assistant and commander of the armies of Israel. Standing at the edge of Jericho, Joshua and the priest, Eleazar, the son of Aaron, whom he succeeded as high priest, were in charge of these wanderers and ready to do the will of the Lord. "He is a man, in whom is the spirit." God said to Moses in Numbers 27:18. He had proved his worth as commander of the armies of Israel in defeating God's enemies, the Amalekites, whom God wiped off the face of the earth. He was ready to meet the Canaanites. First, they had to deal with Jericho. Spies were sent to check out the city and were hidden by Rahab who got them out safely with their promise to save her family when they took over.

An angel of the Lord appeared with directions, and they proceeded to march the armed men around the city once a day for six days. Next, seven priests with trumpets and ram's horns in front of the ark. On the seventh day they marched around the city seven times with the priests blowing the trumpets…then have all the people shout and the walls will fall down. They did, and they took the treasure of the city for the Lord and everything else was burned except for Rahab's family, because of the promise. The place was cursed by God against anyone who would ever rebuild it. The next city they took was Ai.

The covenant was renewed at Shechem. There Joshua copied on stones, the Law of Moses. Then he read to them the whole book of the law. God had instructed that all kings and leaders should do the same periodically, so it would never be forgotten.

Joshua was successful in campaigns in the north and south and defeated the kings of Canaan and now was time to divide the land amongst the tribes.

Not all of the land had been conquered when Joshua was old and unable to do more. It was left for God to deal with, when he and Eleazar died.

PART 7

Judges and the Monarchy to Samuel

After Joshua and Eleazar died the elders were able to continue his program for a time. The tribes became more and more independent from each other. Unity was lost and so was the relationship with God. Though they may have gone through the motions, God was a name and not their leader anymore. In times of trouble they would cry out to him and he would provide a judge to come to their rescue and then they would revert to their independent ways until next time. They reigned in place of kings, for 240 years until Samuel, who was the last Judge and a prophet. Judges were appointed for life and some of them we know only by name and others made a great difference in the path of hope God had prepared for his people Israel. Surrounded by idolatry and terrorism, they suffered, believing that God would always protect them, but only communicating with him when nothing else would work. It is so much like many of us today We use God as a life preserver when the ship is sinking, but ignore him the rest of the time.

God had forsaken them when they did evil and worshipped other gods instead of him and allowed their enemies to pursue them so they would remember the God of their fathers. Then he had compassion on them. He called out Judges to help them.

Othniel of Judah (3:9-11) was the first Judge and he was the Nephew of Caleb. The tribe had been subject to a wicked king for eight years. Their judge, with God's power, went to war and defeated the king and there was peace for 40 years until Othniel died.

Ehud of the tribe of Benjamin (3:15-30) Ehud brought the tribute with a sword hidden under his robes and tricked the king of Moab into sending everyone else away and slew him and left, locking the door behind him. Then he led the Israelites to Moab and killed 10,000 men and took the land. There was peace for 80 years.

Shamgar struck down six hundred Philistines with an ox goad and saved Israel.

Deborah, of the tribe of Ephraim, faced the king, Jabin of Canaan's army under Sisera. He had nine hundred iron chariots and had been harassing Israel for twenty years. Deborah was a prophetess and held court under a tree and sent for Barak to lead ten thousand men against Sisera, but he was afraid and would only go if Deborah led the army. When they got to the place the Lord had promised them victory, Barak led the army and all the enemy troops fell by the sword. Only Sisera escaped to the tent of a Kenite that was a friend, but only the wife, Jael was there. She covered him and he slept She took a hammer and a peg and drove it into his temple. Barak found him there. Israel became strong after this and were able to defeat Jabin. There was peace for forty years. This time two women won the victory.

Again Israel did evil and God gave them for seven years to the power of the Midianites and others who raided their crops, took all they had and drove them into the mountains where they were living in caves. Poverty stricken, they cried out to God.

Gideon of the tribe of Manasseh, of the weakest clan and the least in his family, was called by an angel of God to save Israel. His people were Baal worshipers and God had him take down their altars and build one for God and sacrifice his father's bulls. He did, arousing the town against him. His father said this would test the power of Baal and he could defend himself. So Gideon followed God's instructions and went to save Israel with the power of God upon him. He was a great warrior and all his people followed him and members of other tribes as well. God said he had too many men for God to show his power, so God tested them and got rid of all but 300 men to go against the armies of several kings.

With trumpets and empty jars, with torches inside, he attacked the enemy camp in the middle of the night. There was so much confusion in the camp that they were turning on each other and when others escaped, they pursued them and called back the other tribes to go with them and 120.000 swordsmen fell before them and only about 15,000 were left in hiding. Israel came upon them by surprise and captured them all.

Because of this great victory, the Israelites begged him to be king, but he refused, because God was their king and there was peace for 40 years. He had 71 sons of many wives and died of a good old age.

After Gideon died, his people reverted to the Baals again and his son Abimelech took over and killed all his brothers except Jotham, the youngest, who was able to escape.

Abimelech destroyed Shechem and planned the same fate for Thebez, but a woman dropped a millstone on his head. Then Israel went home in peace.

Tola, of the tribe of Issachar was the next judge, for twenty three years.

Jair, of the tribe of Gilead, judged for twenty two years. He had thirty sons, who controlled thirty towns.

These are called Havoth Jair.

Jephthah was called to judge, when Israel turned to evil once again. God allowed the Philistines and the Ammonites to ravish them for eighteen years, in order to get them to remember him. This judge had been exiled by his brothers because his mother was a prostitute and later called back by the elders because he was a mighty warrior. He defeated their enemies and served them six years.

Ibzan of Judah had thirty sons and thirty daughters. He led Israel seven years

Elon of Zebulun, led Israel ten years.

Abdon, of Ephraim had forty sons and thirty grandsons and led Israel eight years.

Again the Israelites did evil and God gave them over to the Philistines for eighteen years, till they cried out again to God for help. God called a barren woman to conceive a child to be a Nazarite dedicated to God and gave special direction for his upbringing: no haircuts, no wine, special rites of purification and totally consecrated to God.

Samson of the tribe of Dan grew up to be the next Judge. The Lord gave him power to tear apart a lion which attacked him. He married a Philistine woman, which was God's plan to get him to destroy them. She betrayed him and was eventually burned to death with her family by her own people and Samson took revenge on them.

He struck down a thousand men with the jawbone of a donkey.

Chapter sixteen tells the story of Samson and Delilah, a Philistine prostitute who got him to tell the secret of his strength through trickery in order to give him over to her leaders. They gouged out his eyes, shackled him and put him in prison. His hair grew back. All the leaders came to the temple of their God Dagon to celebrate their victory over Samson and brought him to the temple, to humiliate him. He stood between two pillars and clung to them. All the leaders were inside and about three thousand onlookers were on the roof. He prayed and asked God to let him die with the Philistines and in a surge of strength and his arms around the pillars he pulled the temple down and they all died.

Israel once again reverted to other Gods.

RUTH, A GENTILE IN THE FAMILY TREE

The book of Ruth is an important stop on our path of hope for it shows the Lord's compassion on Gentiles (anyone not a Jew).

This is a story of a family who left their brethren during a famine and went to another country which did not recognize their God. Ruth is important to us, because she became the great grandmother of King David and an ancestor of our savior Jesus Christ. It happened in the time of the judges and gives us a glimpse of some who were still faithful to God.

A man named Elimelech and his wife Naomi and their two sons Mahlon and Kilion, left Bethlehem in Judah and went to Moab, who at this time was at peace with Israel. While they lived there, Naomi's husband died and her two sons married Moabite women. About ten years later, both sons also died and she was left a widow with no support and so were her son's wives. They were Orpah and Ruth.

In her despair Naomi knew her only hope was to go back to Israel, so she told the girls to go home and find other husbands and Orpah did so, but Ruth had become attached to Naomi and her God and would not leave her. They went back to Israel together.

Naomi had a relative on her husband's side named Boaz, who was a man of wealth and had huge crops. She sent Ruth to follow the gleaners in his field. They followed the harvesters and picked up the grain that was left. Boaz found out who she was and asked the harvester to leave her extra grain and watch out for her safety. Boaz even invited her to eat with them.

Naomi was interested in finding her a husband and there was a law for a kinsman redeemer to marry a related widow. There was one other closer relation than Boaz, but he refused. Following the custom, she sent Ruth in the middle of the night, to go to Boaz, where he slept. She would cover herself with the hem of his robe as he lay asleep on the threshing floor.

They were married and Boaz became the father of Obed, who fathered Jesse, the father of King David.

SAMUEL, THE LAST JUDGE, AND A PROPHET

When Hannah, a longsuffering, barren, woman's prayers for a child were finally answered, she was so grateful to God that she brought her son, Samuel, to the Priest Eli, as soon as he was weaned, to be raised in his house, dedicated to God's service. Afterward, she had five more children.

God spoke to Samuel, while he was still a boy, but Eli's sons were wicked and abused their place in God's service God. God called Samuel to be a prophet and all Israel listened to him.

Israel was defeated by the Philistines and lost about four thousand men, and soon after, they captured the Ark of God, killing about thirty thousand foot soldiers. Both Eli's sons died on the same day Then Eli died.

The Philistines put the Ark in the temple of their God, Dagon and the next morning their God was on his face before the Ark. They picked him up, but the next day he was down again. His head and hands were broken. As long as the ark remained in their vicinity, they suffered calamities. They removed the Ark from Ashdod to Gath and that city suffered. Then they sent it to Ekron and they suffered too. Then it was sent back to Israel and it remained at Kiriath Jearim for twenty years.

Israel got rid of her false Gods and met with Samuel at Mizpah to consecrate themselves to God once again. The Lord gave them victory over the Philistines. Samuel Judged Israel all his life and appointed his two sons to succeed him, but they were unjust men. Israel would not accept them and asked instead, for a king. God was being rejected and had Samuel tell them all that they would lose if they had a king, but, they persisted.

KING SAUL

They chose Saul, who stood head and shoulders over the other men. Saul, from the tribe of Benjamin, was off chasing his dad's lost donkeys. They sought Samuel to ask his help in locating the animals. Saul met him on the road and he was told, that the animals were already found. He was invited to go along with Samuel to the sacrifice. Saul went and ate with him and stayed the night. In the morning, he would get a message from God. In the morning Samuel gave Saul directions to go to find the prophets who were to meet him. Then he would have the power of God upon him and do what he asked. In seven days they would meet again.

When it was time for him to be anointed, he was hiding among the luggage. Later he rescued the city of Jabesh with three hundred and thirty thousand men, from the Ammonites.

When Saul went to make war against the Philistines, they came out in huge numbers with their iron chariots. They were so many and so powerful that the men with Saul were so afraid, they were looking for places to hide. Saul was supposed to wait for Samuel to come and make the sacrifices to God, that would ensure victory, but, he was so impatient, that when he did not arrive at the appointed time, Saul decided to do it himself, a huge mistake. God required his chosen one to do this service and Saul had no right. Saul had ruled over Israel for forty two years. Now his days were numbered.

By the time Samuel had explained to Saul, that his successor had already been chosen, there were only six hundred of his men left. It was his son Jonathan and his armor bearer who routed the Philistines to confusion, so they were able to bring their army out of hiding and won the day. Then God sent Saul to destroy the Amalakites On the way back he stopped to raise a monument to himself.

God's command was to destroy the Amalakites and everything they had and they had allowed the king, Agag to live and kept all the good stuff. Because Saul had rejected God's command, God rejected him and sent Samuel to Jesse of Bethlehem. He went to make sacrifice, so Saul and Jesse did not know what he was up to.

DAVID-SHEPHERD BOY TO KING

When he had consecrated Jesse and his sons, he sought the one that God had chosen, to replace Saul, and it was none of those with him. He discovered that there was another son tending sheep. It was David and he was to be the next king. Samuel anointed him, and the spirit of the lord came upon him.

Now that God's spirit had left Saul, an evil spirit moved in. His servants searched for someone to play the harp to soothe him and David was chosen. He was soon made an armor bearer and stayed with Saul.

The Philistines came against Israel again with their Champion, the giant Goliath, and taunted Israel to get somebody to fight him, and they trembled in fear. David came on the scene ready to use God's power to defeat this formidable enemy. They tried to get him to wear armor, but he refused and went against the monster with a slingshot and five smooth stones He hit him between the eyes. The giant was dead and David took the sword from him and cut off his head. Israel had conquered the Philistines with a shepherd boy! The army of the Lord chased them back to their cities strewing bodies all the way.

With this awesome deed, David became the champion of Israel and Saul was jealous. Saul's son Jonathan became David's best friend. The evil spirit in Saul took over his every thought. He aimed to kill David and tried to murder him with a sword. Then David went into hiding with Samuel. Jonathan appeased his father and David came back to Saul.

David won more battles with the Philistines and Saul tried to kill him again. Now he sent orders for him to be killed and his wife helped him escape. David once again went with Samuel and stayed with the prophets and when Saul's men came, they prophesied too. Saul went himself and the same spirit came upon him. God protected his anointed.

Jonathan hid him and helped him to escape the anger Saul had also turned on his son. After that Saul slew eighty five priests for siding with David. Saul kept chasing after him and David kept moving. Later Saul had to stop and fight the Philistines, so David was able to escape to another land. When Saul found out where he was, he gathered his army and went after him. Going into a cave where David and his men were hiding, David was able to sneak up and cut off a piece of his robe. David would not harm him because he was anointed by God to be king over him. David confronted Saul with the piece of his robe to prove he was not his enemy and Saul was ashamed of himself, and asked forgiveness and went home.

Samuel died and all Israel mourned for him.

DAVID ON THE RUN

In the desert of Moan, David and his men were in need of food and he sent ten men to ask the rich Calebite, Nabal, who was shearing sheep, to help them. He and his men had not bothered his flocks. Being, a selfish and surly individual, he refused. David and his men prepared to go after Nabal with drawn swords. In the meantime servants of Nabal reported what happened to Nabal's wife, Abigail. She made ready all the supplies needed for David and his men. She set off on a donkey, with her servants, and met David on the way. In the morning, Abigail told her husband what she had done and he had a heart attack, and died a few days later. Afterward, David took her to be his wife.

Saul came after David again and David went into his camp while all were asleep and took Saul's spear and water jug that were by his head.

He went up on the mountain where his voice would echo and called out to Saul's camp. As before, Saul was ashamed and went home.

To avoid Saul, David went to live among the Philistines in Gath with his men and their families. The king, Og of Gath gave him a territory of his own and he lived there over a year, raiding Israel's enemies and leaving no witnesses, so the Philistines thought he was helping them. Then came a time, when the King said he would come with him to attack Israel.

Saul was so afraid that God had left him, that he went to the witch of Endor to ask about his future, even though he had driven all the witches and such out of his country. She was frightened, but he convinced her that he meant her no harm and she cast her spell. When she saw Samuel coming up out of the ground, she screamed in horror, for god had brought the prophet to tell Saul that this was the end of his kingdom and his life and the Philistines would win.

The leaders of the Philistines were suspicious of David and forced the King to send him back. When they arrived in Ziglag, they found it destroyed by the Amalakites, who had taken all the people prisoner. David called upon the Lord and was told to go after them and he did. All that was taken was recovered and the Amalakites defeated.

In the battle between Saul and the Philistines, his sons were killed and he was mortally wounded and fell upon his sword to avoid capture. The Philistines cut off his head and paraded it around their country in triumph.

The Lord sent David and his men to settle in Hebron and while there, men of Judah came to crown him king over their kingdom.

The second book of Samuel is the story of the division of Israel, with David, king in Judah and Saul's son, Ish-Bosheth, king over

Israel, who reigned for two years. David reigned in Judah for seven years and six months. A strange battle occurred, when each side sent twelve young men to fight with daggers, and David's side won the battle. The war between the house of Saul and the kingdom of David lasted a long time. Finally the commander of his opposing forces, Abner, came to David to offer Israel to him. Abner and Saul's son were murdered and David had the perpetrators killed, for these men were innocent. David ruled the united kingdom of Israel for forty years.

He drove the Jebusites out of Jerusalem and made it his city, built a great palace and made Jerusalem a fortress. The Philistines continued to do battle with him, but the Lord continued to give him victory over them.

David chose thirty thousand troops to go with him to bring the Ark of the Covenant to Jerusalem from the house of Abinadab. They brought a new cart and celebrated on the way back that they were bringing the ark of God back to Jerusalem. At one point the oxen stumbled and Uzzah touched the ark and was struck dead, for it was forbidden. God dwelled between the cherubim on top of the ark and he could take care of himself.

David was afraid and took the ark to the house of Obed Edom. It stayed there for three months. When David found that the household had been blessed by its presence, he brought it back to Jerusalem, dancing before the Lord. His wife Michal, daughter of Saul mocked him for it, and she bore no children in all her life.

David wanted to build a house for the Lord, but God spoke to the prophet, Nathan and told him that he had always lived among them in tents and it would be David's son who would build him a house.

David fought and was victorious over all God's enemies and his sons were royal advisers, and he found a son of Jonathan, Maphibosheth, and gave him all the land of his grandfather, Saul, and his servants to work the land. The crippled son of Jonathan ate at the kings table.

In spring the army of Israel was out fighting Ammonites, but David had stayed in Jerusalem. He was walking on the roof of his palace with a keen view of the city before him. Now, David had always lusted after beautiful women and had acquired a large harem of wives, but that did not dull his senses. When he looked down and saw a beautiful woman bathing on her roof with her body glistening in the gloss of the setting sun and her raven hair falling loose beyond her shoulders, he had to have her.

He called his servant to find out about her and she was Bathsheba, the wife of Uriah, the Hittite. David sent for her and slept with her and she became pregnant, while her husband was out fighting in David's army. He decided to cover himself by giving him leave to come home for a visit and he did, but refused to go to his wife when the other men were suffering, while he was away. So, David arranged for him to go to the front lines and be killed, and he was. So he married Bathsheba.

His sin found him out and God was angry with David. He declared, "The sword will never depart from the house of David." The child was born and lived only seven days, but later they had another son and named him, Solomon. The Lord loved him and told the prophet, Nathan, he should be called Jedidiah.

David defeated the Ammonites and made them work with saws, iron, and axes as well as brickmaking.

His son Amnon wanted his half- sister Tamar, and manipulated the situation, so he pretended to be ill and asked for her to bring him food, and he raped her. She was the sister of Absalom who Hated Amnon for what he had done, and she lived in his house. David was furious. Two years later Absalom arranged for his men to kill Amnon at a public occasion. Absalom fled to another country and stayed for three years. Then David sent Joab to bring him home, but would not meet with him.

Four years later, Absalom declared himself king in Hebron, with many followers, and David fled in fear. The Lord had declared that the sword would not depart from his house and he was seeing the result of it, but at the same time the Lord had promised David that the throne would never depart from the House of David.

Absalom led his men against David's men, in the forest, and Absalom's hair caught in a tree and it was easy for the king's men to kill him. David mourned for his son and Absalom had no son.

David returned to Jerusalem and his home. He had met some opposition, but Joab, leading his army took care of it.

Later God became angry with Israel again and David took a census of his fighting men and found, that he had Eight hundred thousand in Israel and Five hundred thousand in Judah. There was no valid reason for him to take a census at this time. He was not about to go to battle with anyone. It may be that he was feeling insecure, now that he was staying in Jerusalem for his own safety while his army was winning wars without his presence, perhaps. God is angry and allows him to choose his own punishment from three options; three years of famine, three months of fleeing from enemies or three days of plague He chose the last and seventy thousand people died. David built an altar to the lord in recompense at God's behest and was forgiven.

PART 8

1-2 Kings From David to Babylon.

David grew old and needed a bed warmer and they found a beautiful girl named Abishag to lie beside him at night and wait on him by day. There was no intimacy.

His son Adonijah, younger brother of Absolum decided he would be king and gathered men to follow him. Joab and the priest Abiathar were with him, but, Zadok the priest was not. The rest of David's elite were not. Nathan, the prophet went to Bathsheba, Solomon's mother, and told her what was going on.

King David sent for his followers and told them to anoint Solomon king and put him on the throne today, and they did. There was great rejoicing in the city and Adonijah was afraid, but Solomon forgave him and sent him home. Shortly after this, David died and Solomon was firmly entrenched as ruler, as he disposed of his father's enemies, even Adonijah, who went to Bathsheba to ask for one of his father's concubines, which would be a part of the kingdom inheritance which went to Solomon. This was a grievous mistake.

He made a treaty with Pharaoh and married his daughter. He also worshiped on the high places, because the Lord had no temple.

Then God spoke to him in a dream and asked what he wished for and he asked for wisdom in leading the people of God. His wish was granted and God promised him wealth besides, and long life if he was obedient.

Solomon was a statesman, he divided his kingdom into twelve districts with their own governors. Each one had to supply provisions for the king's household for one month each year.

The kingdoms round about him had weak kings during the period of his reign and they paid tribute to him and he became very rich. There was peace and prosperity in all his kingdom. He had fortified cities with numerous stables of the finest horses for his troops and iron chariots that outnumbered his enemies. He had more wisdom than any man in the world and was respected by all for his justice.

He built the temple as God said he would. Every part was carefully directed by God himself. Solomon finished it in eleven years and eight months. Then it took thirteen years to build his palace.

There was great celebration, when all Israel gathered to see the priests and the Levites carry the Ark and all the other things from the tent of meeting to the Temple of God, and the glory of God filled the temple in a cloud.

The king blessed the people and gave a prayer of dedication. God came to him again, confirming what he had promised his father David and giving him a warning against worshipping other gods. If that should happen, God would reject him, Israel, and the temple. Solomon would remember this foreboding message all his life.

Solomon built buildings, cities, and a navy and received tribute from many sources, becoming more and more powerful and wealthy. He also made the required sacrifices to the Lord.

The Queen of Sheba came to check out the tales of his wisdom and his God, bringing many gifts from her own country, in a great caravan, and she was pleased to find he was far greater than what she had expected. There are legends that say he had an affair with her, but such was not reported in the scriptures.

As Solomon's riches grew, he married many foreign women. God had forbidden Israel to do so, because they would pollute the nation with other gods and cause them to stray from the one true God to worship them.

He had seven hundred wives of royal birth and three hundred concubines. As he grew old he gave in to their pleas and began to worship with them and honor their gods along with God. His sin would change everything for Israel.

The foreboding message, from God's last visit, was like a sword hanging over their heads. God lowered it by proclaiming that Solomon's kingdom would fall when he died and a son would get one tribe, to keep his promise in covenant with David, his father. God would always have a remnant for new beginnings. Israel was never left without hope.

God raised up an adversary, against David, Hadad the Edomite. Joab, the commander of David's army had killed all the Edomite men. Hadad was only a boy and had escaped to Egypt.

Another rebel from long ago destruction, Rezon, who ruled in Aram and led forces against Solomon all his life. Another enemy was one of his own officials. His name was Jeroboam, an Ephraimite.

Jeroboam was told by a prophet, that he would be given ten tribes by God, upon the death of Solomon. He fled to Egypt to be safe until the king died.

Upon his father's demise, Rehoboam became king. All the people refused him except Judah. All the rest went with Jeroboam.

Jeroboam did not want to compete with the house of David, so he made two golden calves and set them up in two different places and told his people to worship them.

As he was bringing sacrifices to the heathen gods, God sent his own man from Judah to curse the altar and the man. When Jeroboam told his men to seize him and reached out his hand, God caused it to shrivel up and he could not move it. The alter split in two, and the ashes poured out. God promised a son of the house of David, named Josiah, would annihilate the perpetrators of this abomination.

Jeroboam continued to disobey God and when his son was sick, he sent his wife, in a disguise to Ahijah, the prophet to find out what would happen to his son.

God promised disaster to Jeroboam. His son would die, when his mother entered the city. All who followed him would die and his home would burn and he would have nothing left, because he was an evil man. Israel will suffer exile because of his sin. He served Israel twenty two years and his son, Nadab became king of Israel.

Solomon's son Rehoboam was king in Judah for seventeen years and did evil in the eyes of the Lord. The people had become like the Canaanites that were there in the land before them.

Shishak, king of Egypt attacked Jerusalem and took all the treasures of Judah which Solomon had collected and Rehoboam had to use bronze instead of gold. He continued to war against Israel until he died and his son Abijah replaced him. He reigned for three years. When he died, His son Asa took the throne and reigned forty one years. Finally this family had produced a God fearing man who aimed to please the Lord. He united with the king of Aram and defeated Israel, who was still warring against him.

Baasha had become king in Israel upon the demise of Abijah, his father. God destroyed him and his followers and raised up Jehu the prophet to deliver his ultimatum. It came to pass, that he met the same fate as Jeroboam. Elah, son of Baasha, became king and reigned two years. Zimri, an official in the king's court, assassinated him and took his place. Destroying all Baasha's family and friends gave him an advantage, so he thought.

When he had been king for seven days, the army, commanded by Omri, rose up against him and chose their leader as king. They took the city and Zimri set the palace on fire and died. Omri became king and reigned for twelve years. He built a new capital city on the hill of Shemar in Samaria and was more, wicked than his predecessors. He was followed by his son, Ahab, who was worse than his father. He ruled Israel for twenty two years.

AHAB THE KING AND ELIJAH THE PROPHET

God raised up a prophet in Israel named Elijah, from the tribe of Gilead to keep the king in line. God's message for Ahab was that there would be no rain or dew for years, and it would only come at God's command. Then he sent Elijah away to hide from Ahab to a place where he would drink from a brook and be fed by ravens. When the brook dried up, God sent him to Zarephath and appointed a widow to look after him.

She had only a little flour in a jar and a little oil, but all the time Elijah stayed there it never ran out. She had no hope for herself and her son, but because she was obedient to God, she, her son and Elijah

47

were able to survive. Later the child was sick and died. Elijah cried out to the Lord and the child lived.

In three years, God sent Elijah back to Ahab to tell him that rain was coming. At the same time God had a man named Obediah working in the palace. Jezebel, Ahab's heathen wife, was killing God's prophets. This man was hiding a hundred of them in caves. Elijah met Obediah on his way and sent a message to Ahab to come and meet him at a certain place.

God's message for Ahab was to bring all his people and all his false prophets to meet with Elijah on Mount Carmel. There he would challenge their god. They would bring bulls for sacrifice on each of their altars. The bulls were prepared as usual and Elijah announced that whichever altar was set afire would reveal the true God. The heathens prayed to their gods untill noon and not a spark was seen. They were shouting and dancing around their altar in a frenzy and Elijah was mocking them the whole time. They were even slashing themselves and blood was streaming down. But their gods did not respond.

Elijah called out to them to come and watch him, as he dug a ditch around his altar. He asked them to bring water in four jars three times and pour it over the parts of the bull and the wood. So, they were saturated and it was running into the ditch. Then Elijah cried out to God to send fire from heaven and it came and burned the offering and the wood, the stones and the dirt. It even lapped up the water in the ditch. All the people fell on their faces before the one true God.

The four hundred and fifty prophets of Baal were seized and slaughtered. Elijah sent Ahab home and went to the top of the mountain to pray for the rain to come and it did, as God had promised.

Jezebel promised to see him as dead as her prophets. She sent messengers all over the country to make sure Elijah knew his days were numbered and he fled in fear to hide in the desert. When he was unable to run anymore, he laid down under a Broom tree and fell asleep. He was awakened by and angel, who gave him food and water. Later he came back and did it again. After that, in the strength of God's power for his weakness, he was able to travel for forty days and forty nights. When he came to mount Horeb, the mountain of God, he took shelter in a cave.

God came and asked him why he had run away and he said he was afraid for his life because he was the only prophet left and he would surely be found and put to death like the rest. Then God ordered him to stand on the mountain top, where he would pass by. When he obeyed, a wild, and destructive wind passed by, but God was not there. (A tornado). God was still not there when there was an earthquake. Then there was fire and after that a soft whisper and God was there. (A moment with God makes it necessary that we have to have a quiet time to listen carefully to that still, small voice of our Lord. He is too gentle to shout. We have to pay attention or distractions might cause us to miss it.)

Now Elijah was listening carefully. He covered his face and cowered in the front of the cave. The Lord told him to go to the desert of Damascus and anoint three men: Hazael to be king over Aram and Jehu to be king in Israel and Elisha to replace Elijah. He also said he had seven thousand faithful men in Israel.

Elijah followed the instructions he had been given and found Elisha plowing a field. He threw his cloak around him and he became his follower, attending to his needs.

The king of Aram and thirty two other kings and their armies and chariots went to war on Samaria. Ben Hadad of Aram went against

Ahab of Israel. The Lord sent a prophet to Ahab and told him how to win the battle and Ahab obeyed the Lord and defeated his enemies. In the spring, the king of Aram and his cohorts tried again to defeat Israel, but the man of God came again to give Ahab directions and the result was this; "The Israelites inflicted a hundred thousand casualties on their foot soldiers, in one day. The rest of them escaped to the city of Aphek, where the wall collapsed on twenty thousand of them, and Ben Hadad fled to the city and hid in an inner room." (1 Kings 20:29....30) Ben Hadad came to Ahab begging for his life. He made a treaty and sent him home. God was angry, because Ben Hadad was his enemy and should die for his wickedness, now Ahab would die and lose his position.

An incident took place that changed things, for a while. Ahab wanted the vineyard of his neighbor, Naboth, and the man would not give up the land of his forefathers. When Ahab sulked over it, Jezebel, his wife told him she would get it for him. She arranged for Naboth to be killed with false witness against him and Ahab was happy again.

God sent Elijah to convict him of the crime and cursed him for it, but Ahab humbled himself and God put the curse on the next generation. Then there were three years of peace. After that, Ahab went against Ramoth Gilead without God's blessing and was killed.

Jehoshaphat, king of Judah was with him in this endeavor. Now Ahab's son, Ahaziah would take the throne of Israel and suffer the curse put on his father's house, because of Naboth's murder. He was just like his father, an evil man.

Jehoshaphat ruled in Judah twenty five years. He was a good king like his father Asa. When he died he was replaced by his son, Jehoram.

Moab came against Israel and Ahaziah fell and was injured so he could not go. He sent a messenger to Baalzebub his God to see if he would get better. God sent Elijah to meet the messenger and told him that God had said he would surely die.

Ahaziah sent a Captain and fifty men to bring Elijah to him. Elijah called down fire from heaven and destroyed them. When they did not return, the king sent another group after the prophet. The same thing happened again. When the third contingent appeared, the captain fell on his face before Elijah and begged for his life and God directed him to go with them. The prophet repeated what the Lord God had said. Then the king died. He had no son, so Joram took the throne.

Elijah and Elisha were traveling together and when they stopped at the Jordan River he threw his cloak over the water and it parted for them to pass over. There was a group of prophets there, and they all knew that Elijah was going to be taken up by God.

On the other side Elijah asked if he could do anything for his companion before he went up and Elisha had one request. "Let me inherit a double portion of your spirit." (2 Kings 9b) Elijah said that if he saw him being taken up, he would have it. Soon after, he saw Elijah being taken up in a whirlwind in a chariot of fire, with horses of fire. He got his wish. After he had disappeared, Elisha took Elijah's cloak, which had fallen and went to the Jordan and struck the water. When it parted, he crossed over.

ELISHA THE PROPHET

He went to a city where the water was polluted and the land was not good for crops. He took salt and threw it in the spring and told them that the water and the land would always be good from now on.

Joram, son of Ahab reigned twenty years over Israel and was evil, in the eyes if the Lord. But, when Moab rose up against Israel, Jehoshaphat, king of Judah, and the king of Edom joined forces with him and the Lord blessed them. The Moabites were sorely defeated and their land polluted.

Elisha was called upon by the widow of a prophet. She was having a problem with her deceased husband's creditors. They wanted to take her sons as slaves, in payment for his debts. He told her to collect empty jars and fill them from her little bit of oil and she filled every jar she could find and then sold the oil to pay the debts. God has promised to supply all our needs.

Elisha went to Shunem and there was a family there who kept a room for him whenever he came there. They had no son. He prayed and God gave them one. Later their son became ill and died and the mother came and cried out to Elisha. He went home with her and went to the boy's room and shut the door. He prayed and lay prostrate over the child's body and it began to warm. He prayed more and did it a second time and he came back to life.

Elisha went back to Gilgal and met with the company of prophets during a famine. A pot of stew was made from gathering things from the field and it was tainted and the men who tasted it cried out to Elisha. He added some flour to it and it was fine.

A man came to donate twenty loaves of Barley bread to the prophet and Elisha told him to give it to the people, but there were one hundred men. He said that there would be enough and some left over, because the Lord said so. Elisha had inherited twice the spirit of his predecessor Elijah.

Naaman was a great hero in Aram, where he commanded the army. When he got leprosy. A slave girl from Israel, told her master about the prophet in Samaria. The king sent a message to the king of Israel asking for his warriors healing.

When Naaman reached Elisha's house he was given a message to go wash seven times in the Jordan River. He went away afire with wrath. It was not what he expected. After a while his servants calmed him down and he obeyed the prophet. He was instantly healed. Overjoyed at the results, Naaman went back to reward Elisha, but the prophet would not accept anything. Naaman promised to never worship any other God, but the God of Elisha.

Gehazi, the prophet's servant, seized the opportunity to gain something for himself. He ran after Naaman and lied to get silver and clothing for himself, saying his master had sent him. Gehazi returned and hid his treasure and was shocked when his master knew what he had done. He was awarded for his treachery with the gift of Naaman's leprosy for himself and his descendants, and was immediately stricken.

Elisha and the company of prophets went to the Jordan to build a larger place for them to meet. They began to cut down trees and an iron axe head fell into the water. Elisha cut a stick and threw it into the water to make the axe head float and it was retrieved.

The king of Aram went to war against Israel and Elisha reported their every movement to the king. Aram was inflamed at the prophet over this and when they surrounded him, the Lord struck them blind at his request. Elisha told them that they were in the wrong place and led them to Samaria and they stood before the king of Israel and received their sight. Elisha had a feast prepared for them and then sent them home. Aram decided not to bother Israel anymore.

Much later King Ben Hadad, king of Aram stormed the city of Samaria. A famine ensued and a donkey cost a fortune and people were turning to cannibalism. The King was beside himself and blamed Elisha for bringing this disaster on them.

When he went with his men after him, Elisha gave them the word of the Lord for this situation. He said that food would sell for reasonable prices at the gate of the city on the very next day. When it happened according to prophecy, the king's officer, who had mocked the prophet, was killed in the stampede for food.

Four men with leprosy were there before, and knew that they were going to die. They decided to go to the Arameans where there was food and perhaps they would have pity on them. If not, they would die anyway. When they arrived there the Arameans heard a noise and thought an onslaught of kings had come after them, and they fled with great haste, leaving everything in the camp intact for them to enjoy. They went back to report to the king of their discovery and this was where the food came from. The God of hope was still in business.

Elisha had told the family of the boy he had raised from the dead, to go away and live in another country for seven years, because the famine was coming and would last that long. They moved to the land of the philistines and came back when the seven years were up. They went to the king and pleaded with him to give them back the home and land that they had left. When he found out that the boy with them had been raised from the dead by Elisha, he gave it all back, including all the income that had been made while they were away.

Elisha went to Damascus when King Ben Hadad was dying and was met by a man named Hazeal, bringing him gifts. There were forty camel loads. Elisha told the man to tell his master that he would get well, but said he would surely die. Elisha wept because he knew Hazeal would become king and do great harm to Israel. The man gave his king the positive message and then Hazeal smothered the king and took the throne of the land of Aram.

When Joram, son of Ahab, was king of Israel and Jehoram, son of Jehoshaphat, was king in Judah, Jehoram was like the evil kings of Israel. He was even married to a daughter of Ahab. God would not destroy Judah, because of his promise to David; that it would last forever. Edom rebelled and became independent. Libnah did the same. When he died, his son Ahaziah took the throne.

This king joined with Joram, the king of Israel to war against Hazael, king of Aram. Jorom was wounded and Ahaziah followed him home. He only reigned one year.

Elisha sent one of the company of prophets to anoint Jehu, commander of the army, king in Israel, secretly, and then run. He followed these instructions, anointed the man's head with oil and gave him God's message. God would annihilate the house of Ahab and destroy all things connected to it, in revenge for all the evils of Ahab and Jezebel, and he opened the door and ran for his life.

Jehu's first accomplishment was to slay Joram and Hazael, kings of Israel and Aram at God's command. Then they killed Ahaziah, king of Judah. Then they went after Jezebel. The officials in the city sent the heads of Ahab's seventy sons to Jehu to prove their loyalty to him. When Jehu reached the place that housed Jezebel, the eunuchs threw her down and when they came to bury her, they found that the dogs had left only her skull, her feet and her hands, just as the prophet Elijah had prophesied. All of Ahab's family and coconspirators were gone, just as promised. He also killed all the priests of Baal.

When Jehu died, his son Jehoahaz was king over Israel. And he reigned twenty eight years.

The mother of Ahaziah was so affected by the death of her son that she attempted to kill off all the royal family. Only Joash, son of Ahaziah, was able to escape. After she had killed the rest of the family, Athaliah ruled while the boy hid for six years. At that time Israel was ripe for change.

Jehoiada the priest, who with his wife, had protected him from Athaliah, brought him forth and presented him to the people and anointed him king. Athaliah was put to death. Joash was given a copy of the covenant. He reigned in Jerusalem for forty years. The priest had made a covenant with the Lord, the king and the people, that the people of Israel would be true to God and the covenant. God had redeemed the people of Judah from their evil ways. Hope was once again renewed.

They restored the temple of the Lord. Then Hazael, king of Aram came to attack Jerusalem, after he had already captured Gath. Joash sent him all the treasure in the temple and the palace and he went away. At the last, his officials murdered him and Amaziah, his son took his place.

In the twenty third year of Joash, Jehoahaz, son of Jehu became king in Israel for seventeen years. He did evil in the eyes of the Lord. God allowed them to be ruled by the king of Aram and his son for many years. Then Jehoahaz cried out to the Lord and he sent a deliverer to Israel.

The king died and his son Jehoash took the throne of Israel and drove out Aram. He ruled for sixteen years doing evil as his forefather's had done. He was replaced by Jeroboam II.

At this time, the prophet Elisha died and the king had come and wept over the man of God. Elisha had a message for him. "You will completely destroy the Arameans." But because he did not beat the ground in the way he was directed, he would only defeat them three times.

THE DIVIDED KINGDOM

During the reign of Jehoash in Israel, Amaziah became king in Judah. He ruled for twenty nine years. He executed the officials who had killed his father. He also defeated ten thousand Edomites. He warred against Israel and was captured and the wall of Jerusalem was broken down. All the treasures of the city were taken and with hostages was removed to Israel. He was allowed to remain on the throne for fifteen years and was then killed in a conspiracy.

While he was king, in Israel, Jeroboam 11 was king in Judah. He ruled for forty one years and did evil against the Lord. He restored the boundaries of his kingdom. He also recovered both Damascus and Hamath. When he died, Zechariah, his son replaced him. He was murdered six months later, in public, by his successor, Shallum, who only lasted one month. Then he was killed by Menahem, who took his place. He did evil all through his reign in Judah. He was forced to pay tribute to Assyria. Pekahiah, his son followed his father as king. Over Israel. He reigned for two years and was murdered by Pekah, another evil king who reigned for twenty years in Israel.

Tiglath-Pileser King of Assyria at this time took over Ijon, Abel Beth Maacah, Janoah, Kedesh and Hazor, Gilead and Galilee. He also took all the territory of Naphtali and sent all the people to Assyria. Then, Hoshea, son of Elah killed Pekah and became king in Israel.

Jotham, son of Azariah was king in Judah. He ruled for sixteen years. He was a good king and his son, Ahaz followed him as king. He ruled sixteen years and did not please the lord. He even sacrificed his son in the fire of a foreign god. Rezin, king of Aram drove Judah out of Elath and Edomites took it over. Then Assyria took Damascus and sent its people to Kir and killed king Rezin.

Ahaz, King in Judah was followed by his son Hezekiah.

Hoshea was the last king in Israel. After years of paying tribute to Assyria, they stopped and the Assyrians took all of Israel into captivity. They had rejected the Lord, their God and now, God rejected them,

Hezakiah ruled Judah in Jerusalem for twenty nine years. He cleansed his kingdom of all remnants of idolatry. Repaired the temple, which had been neglected and polluted for years under evil kings. He also reinstated the Passover.

When, Sennacherib, the king of Assyria captured his fortified cities, he offered to pay tribute to save the rest. The Assyrians called on them to surrender and mocked the God of Judah. Hezekiah called on the prophet Isaiah to help them.

He told them not to be afraid, because he would take care of the Assyrians. Hezekiah went to his knees and called out to God in his distress and that night God answered. After dark, in the Assyrian camp, one hundred and eighty five thousand men died. Sennacherib went home in defeat and bothered Judah no more. Afterward, he was killed by his own sons.

Envoys from the king of Babylon came to visit Hezekiah in Judah. He was so proud of all his holdings, he even showed them all his treasures. Afterward, God spoke through Isaiah, the prophet to warn him of the mistake he had made. The Lord said that sometime in the future, Babylon would come and take everything he had and Judah would be taken in captivity to Babylon. One of his great achievements was a water system into the city. When he died, the throne passed to his son, Manasseh.

Manasseh ruled for fifty five years. He brought back the idol worship that his father had banned and rebuilt all the high places and altars as before, even the house of the Lord. He sacrificed his son in the fire and practiced sorcery. When he died, Amon, his son, took his place. He was just like his father, evil in all his ways. He ruled for two years and was murdered by palace officials. Then the people killed the king's enemies and put his son, Josiah on the throne. He reigned for thirty one years. He walked in the ways of the Lord.

KING JOSIAH AND THE BOOK

During the reign of Josiah, a priest found The Book of the Law (Deuteronomy) when the temple was being restored. He read it and then gave it to the king to read. He sent for Huldah a prophetess who remembered the book and told them its message.

Josiah read the book to the people and sent them to destroy all traces of idolatry in the kingdom. The people were now commanded to worship the one true God. He renewed the covenant with God and the people. He was a better King than the others before him. He was killed in a battle with Neco of Egypt and his son, Jehoahaz, ruled Judah for three months. Pharaoh Neco put him in chains and he died in Egypt Then he replaced him with Josiah's son, Eliakim and changed his name to Jehoiakim. Judah would now pay tribute to Neco by taxing the people. He ruled eleven years, doing evil in the eyes of the Lord.

PART 9

Babylon Rules

Nebuchadnezzar, king in Babylon took over and made him pay tribute for three years. Then he refused. God sent Babylon, Aram, and Moab against Judah. The sins of the past and present had sealed their fate, just as the prophets had predicted.

The king died and was replaced by his son, Jehoiachin. He only lasted three months. The king of Babylon captured him and his whole family. He took all the wealth of Jerusalem and ten thousand of the best citizens into captivity, and left only the poorest of the population. God put his uncle Zedekiah on the throne. He ruled eleven years. Then, he rebelled against Babylon.

In the ninth year of his reign. The king of Babylon and his army laid siege to Jerusalem and kept pounding it for two years. There was no food left and their army broke down a wall and ran away, but were killed. The king was tortured. His sons were killed, his eyes gouged out and he was taken prisoner to Babylon. The walls of the city were leveled and the most important buildings and homes were burned and only the poorest were left to the vineyards and fields.

A governor was placed over the ones left in Judah and a few months later, the men of Judah killed him and fled to Egypt. After Jehoiachin had been in Babylon thirty seven years there was a new king. He released his prisoner and brought him to eat at his table for the rest of his life.

PART 10

Ezra returns From Exile

Cyrus, King in Persia, ruler over Babylon made a decree that all of the exiles who wished to return to Jerusalem and rebuild the temple were free to go. Their neighbors were to supply all their needs to honor their God, who had given him "all the kingdoms of the earth. He also ordered that all the treasure that had been taken from the house of the Lord would be returned to Jerusalem in Judah. The number that left Babylon under Cyrus was forty two thousand, plus seven thousand three hundred and thirty seven servants.

They settled in their towns and seven months later met together in Jerusalem and the priests and others began to build the altar for burnt offerings. Then they celebrated the feast of tabernacles. Everyone made offerings of money as they were able to start rebuilding the temple, and construction was begun. They bought materials from Sidon and Tyre, and cedar across the sea from Lebanon. When the foundation was finished, the people gathered together to worship, sing and shout praises to the Lord. Some were weeping.

Zerubbable, Jeshua, and the heads of families rejected offers of help from God's enemies. The people around them continued to harass them and tried to make them stop the building program.

When Artaxerxes became king in Persia, he was influenced by his own staff and other countries round about that Jerusalem had been destroyed because it had become dangerous to their welfare. It should not be allowed to be restored.

He sent men to stop the work and it was halted until King Darius took the throne of Persia many years later. Haggai and Zechariah, prophets of God began to urge the men to start the building project again. With Gods prophets behind them they began again. Complaints again came to the throne of Persia.

Darius gave them permission to continue to restore their temple. He even took money from the royal treasury to supply all their needs. He also decreed that if anyone went against his orders, his house would be destroyed. It was completed in six years and the Jews prospered because of Darius.

Everything was carried out according to God's plan and the priests and Levites were installed in their original positions. There was a joyous celebration attended by all the exiles and the proper sacrifices were made. From that day forward all the holy days would be restored to them.

Later during the reign of Artaxerxes, who ruled in Persia for forty years, Ezra the priest came from Babylon to Jerusalem as a teacher of the Law of Moses and was God's man for his time. The king sent many other exiles back: fifteen hundred men, thirty eight Levites, and two hundred and twenty helpers.

Ezra was given all he would need for his journey and his living, as well as gifts for God. Also Ezra was to appoint judges and magistrates over his people. The king also warned all of his kingdom to supply the needs of Ezra and the servants of the "God of heaven" and threatened anyone who bothered the Jews, with severe punishment.

Ezra was told of the sins of the exiles in marrying the peoples around them, who had evil practices in the eyes of the Lord their God. Ezra went to the house of the Lord and prostrated himself on the floor and cried out to God in his torment for their sin. He tore his clothes and pulled out his hair and beard in penitence, knowing something must be done to purify the remnant that was left of God's people. A crowd had gathered around him and wept with him for their sin. They repented and said, "There is still hope for Israel." Then they made a covenant to send away their foreign wives and their children. A Jew has to have a mother that is a Jew. Ezra heard their oath to do what must be done and withdrew to a room in the house of a friend and prayed and fasted for his brethren.

All the men who had married foreign wives had to meet before a judge to evaluate each individual case and anyone who refused to comply with the covenant, would be sent into exile.

PART 11

---◇---

Nehemiah Builds a Wall

He was cupbearer to the king of Persia. When his brother returned from a trip to Jerusalem, he reported on the poverty there and the fact that the walls were still broken down and the gates were burned. This brought great sorrow to Nehemiah and he prayed for a solution. He went to the king and explained the situation his countrymen were in and asked for permission to go and help them. His wish was granted on condition that he would return after a certain time.

He left Persia accompanied by army officers and cavalry with letters to all He also carried a letter to the governors whose lands he would pass through. He was also given a letter to the keeper of the king's forest, for timber he would need for the rebuilding.

Sanballat the Horonite, and Tobiah an Ammonite official were upset that the building up of Jerusalem was going to take place. They were joined by Gershem, an Arab in mocking and making trouble for the builders, trying to stop their work.

The priests repaired and dedicated the Sheep Gate and had a dedication ceremony. Other builders began on each side of it. The project was underway all around Jerusalem. When the wall had reached half its height, their enemies began to attack them. At the same time, the builders were running out of strength, and there were piles of rubble in the way.

Nehemiah posted half the men as armed guards around the wall and the workers wore their swords to protect themselves from a potential attack. When the wall was finished, Nehemiah took a census and then the families went to their own towns.

Ezra was called to read the book of the law at a gathering of all the people. He read the book from sunrise till noon and the people were pleased. They all stood with raised hands and said Amen and bowed their faces to the ground in worship. Then the Levites explained the scriptures to them. It was a sacred day. The people went away with great joy. Soon after, they celebrated the feast of booths, which they had not done since the time of Joshua. Every day Ezra read from the book of the law for seven days.

All the foreigners had left and they celebrated that they were now back in God's will moving around their country, with leaders living in Jerusalem and assigning duties to people who would be responsible for the House of God and caring for provisions and all the things that make a capital city run smoothly. All the time, they were being reminded of what God had done for them and rebuking the evil behavior of their forebears.

It came time, for Nehemiah to return to his duties in Persia. Later on he was allowed to go back for a visit. He found that they had turned back to their old ways: neglecting the house of the Lord, not keeping the Sabbath holy, and even marrying foreign, wives. He did his best to straighten them out, crying out to God for his brethren in Judah.

PART 12

Esther, The girl who saved her people

This story took place before Ezra came back to Jerusalem with the exiles.

King Xerxes of Persia gave a banquet for his officials and friends in his palace at Susa for seven days. On the last day being high on much wine, he called for Queen Vashti to come and show off her exquisite beauty. She was holding a banquet for the ladies while he was entertaining the men. The messengers came back to report that the Queen refused to come to him. He was furious and after conferring with his advisers he sent a message to her with direction to leave her position and never again come into the presence of the king.

After that, it was necessary to find a replacement for the Queen. A squad of men was sent to every province in the kingdom. They were commanded to find the most beautiful virgins and bring them back to the king's harem. There they were to receive six months of treatment with oils and another six months of perfumes and cosmetics, before they could go and spend a night with the king.

One of these young virgins was a Jewess named Esther (no one knew of her origin except her uncle Mordecai, who lived in the city). When her turn arrived, she found favor with her king. He put a crown on her head and pronounced her Queen.

Haman was an important man in the palace and he had earned the right to be honored by the populace. Mordecai refused to bow down to him and this inspired passionate wrath in this arrogant man.

He hated Mordecai and his people and devised a plan to rid himself of the lot of them. He went to the king with lies about their behavior toward the king and laid out an edict to get rid of the trouble makers.

The king agreed and signed the document that would have every Jew in every province killed on a certain day. It was sent immediately to every part of the kingdom

Mordecai found out about it and warned his people and sent a message to Esther to go to the king and plead their cause. She sent a message back to her uncle explaining that if she went into the inner court without being summoned by the king, it would mean certain death. The only thing that would save her, would be if the king extended his scepter, giving her permission to come to him.

Mordecai warned her that she would be killed anyway when they found out she was a Jew, herself. She realized that she had to risk her life, because there was no other way to save her people.

She went into the inner court with much trepidation and stood there until the king noticed her. He extended his scepter and asked what she needed and he would give it to her, even half his kingdom. She said she wanted to prepare a banquet for him and Haman. He was surprised, but pleased and would send for the man immediately to invite him.

Haman was excited to receive such an invitation from the queen and went about crowing about being in her favor. He was also gloating about the fact that he was getting revenge on Mordecai the Jew for his insults. He had even built a gallows awaiting the appointed day.

That night, the king could not sleep and got up and looked through his journals and found an account of a time when Mordecai, the Jew had overheard a plot being planned to kill the king and had reported it. It was found to be true and the criminals were put to death. He also noted that the man had never been honored for his deed.

The next day he called on Haman for advice and he asked him how he would honor a man who had done great service for the king. Haman thought that this man must be him and called for lavish gifts and a marvelous parade through the city streets

When the time came for the banquet and they were settled in the great hall, the king asked again what he could do for his Queen and she related the situation between Haman and Mordecai and the reason for the edict to kill all the Jews. The king was so incensed over what this man had done, that he ordered him to be hanged on his own gallows. His estate was given to the queen and she gave her uncle charge over it and he became an important man in the palace of the king.

The king's edict could not be revoked so he made another one. It allowed the Jews to kill all their enemies at the time he had set to kill the Jews and all the people feared them. They succeeded in ridding themselves of their enemies and lived in peace afterward.

PART 13

---✦---

Job, Lost all but His Faith

Job was a very rich man who found favor with God and the devil mocked God, saying, this man would not be so good if God did not have a fence around him. God assured him, that he would stay faithful under any circumstances. He allowed the devil to do what he wished except he could not take his life.

Job lost his children, his property and possessions. His body was covered with painful sores. He could not understand why God would put him through such testing, when he knew no reason for punishment.

His friends came to console him and reached the conclusion that there had to be sin in his life. His nagging wife said, "Curse God and die." God rebuked his friends and restored to Job more than he ever had before. While he was falling apart with grief, God spoke to him and brought him out of it with compassion and love. The word hope is used in Job 18 times.

PART 14

Psalms-Man speaking to God

The book of Psalms contains Psalms of praise and hymns. There are 150 and 73 are attributed to King David. Moses wrote Psalm 90. Solomon wrote 72 and 127. Heman wrote psalm 88. Ethan wrote Psalm 89. Asaph did 50, and 73-80. The sons of Korah did psalms 42, and 44-49, 84, 85 and 87. 49 are anonymous.

Psalm 2 is a portrayal of the Messish, redeemer and king, Jesus the Christ of God.

Psalm 110 portrays him as our forever priest.

Psalm 16 predicts resurrection.

Psalm 72 predicts the millennial reign

We use many of the psalms today. For instance, the 23rd psalm is often used at funerals. Psalm 92 is uplifting for old folks. Psalm 27 is helpful for the fearful etc.

They are separated into five books and contain the word hope 30 times.

PART 15

Proverbs, Warnings to the Young

This book was probably written by Solomon but some of the last were attributed to the wise, who might have gotten their words from Solomon. They are written for young men, given as a roadmap to a good life. Solomon, when he was old, had many regrets that had made him a very unhappy man at the end of his life. The message to a son, in these passages, makes it very personal. They deal with the usual behavior of young men, especially with sexuality. Sexual sin is not only a sin against your own body, but a sin against God. He says clearly, "Rejoice in the wife of thy youth." (Pr. 5:18)

The purpose of the whole book is given in the very beginning.

CHAPTER 1

For attaining wisdom and discipline; for understanding words of insight; for acquiring a disciplined and a prudent life doing what is right and just and fair; for giving prudence to the simple, knowledge and discretion to the young. Let the wise listen and add to their learning. Let the discerning get guidance-for understanding proverbs and parables, the sayings and riddles of the wise. The fear of the Lord is the beginning of knowledge but fools despise wisdom and discipline.

PART 16

Ecclesiastes, Life is Meaningless

This too is Solomon, philosophizing about life in general. It is all meaningless. In some versions of the Bible it is referred to as vanity. In the end he gives hope by pointing to God as the answer to all of life's problems.

1. Everything is meaningless. 2. Wisdom is meaningless. 3. Pleasures are meaningless. 4. A time for everything: A time to be born and a time to die. A time to plant and a time to uproot. A time to kill and a time to heal. A time to tear down and a time to build. A time to weep and a time to laugh. A time to mourn and a time to dance. A time to scatter stones and a time to gather them. A time to embrace and a time to refrain. A time to search and a time to give up. A time to keep and a time to throw away. A time to tear and a time to mend. A time to be silent and a time to speak. A time to love and a time to hate. A time for war and a time for peace. 5. Oppression, toil, friendlessness 6. Advancement is meaningless. 7. Stand in awe of God. 8. Wisdom 9. A common destiny for all 10. Bread upon the waters.

He ends with this. For God will bring every deed into judgment, including every hidden thing, whether it is good or evil.

Man may try to play God and solve all his own problems. He may even dabble in science and try to figure out how God created the universe, but only God has the answers to every question. All our hope is in the creator, the light of the world, as we walk about in chaos and confusion.

PART 17

Isaiah, Prince of Prophets

Isaiah-the greatest prophet of the Old Testament served the Lord in Jerusalem for forty years, under four kings. He is known as the greatest writing prophet, for he wrote not only the book that bears his name, but also wrote the biographies of two kings. He is also called a messianic prophet, because he prophecies the coming of Jesus and his life here, his death and resurrection and his return in glory to reign for a thousand years.

From the beginning, the people resisted the things of God and paid no attention to his pleas for them to return to his favor. Most of his prophesy came to be of Judgment and salvation. The future was foreboding, with long years of hardship and exile to foreign nations, but he also gave them hope that there would come a time in future generations that they could find forgiveness and return to their homeland.

Later on as some of his prophecies came true. People began to pay attention.

Israel was deteriorating and the Assyrians were gaining more power. He predicted the end of Judah and Israel and the remnant that would be true to the living God. In the end these prophecies did come true exactly as he said. Even Cyrus the Persian was influenced to let God's people go, after he had conquered Babylon, because of Isaiah.

He retired during Hezekiah's reign and was sawn in half during the reign of Manasseh.

Isaiah 40:31…But, those who hope in the Lord, will renew their strength. They will soar on wings like eagles. They will run and not grow weary. They will walk and not be faint.

PART 18

Jeramiah, the Weeping Prophet

He was called by God as a very young man from the tribe of Benjamin. His father was a pagan priest and his family and their neighbors persecuted him, so he fled to Jerusalem. He served the Lord for forty years, under five kings. There were good kings and bad kings, but his reception was never good among the people. He was a priest of God and a prophet of doom, for they would not turn back to the one true God.

When it became dangerous for him to even go to the house of the Lord, he had a scribe named Baruch who became his constant companion. He wrote down all the words that Jeremiah dictated. Then he would read them in public and even to the king.

King Jehoiakim took the scrolls from Baruch and destroyed them. The next thing he did was to order both **Baruch and Jeramiah to be arrested.** They were able to escape his wrath.

When King Zedekiah was in league with Egypt for protection from the King of Babylon, the Pharaoh's army had gone home and the army of Babylon was coming closer in force. He had called on Jeremiah to get a message from God about this perilous situation.

Jeremiah gave him a message he did not want to hear. God said that Jerusalem would be defeated and burned.

Jeremiah had to leave the city on business and was stopped at the Benjamin gate. He was accused of going over to the Babylonians. He was beaten and imprisoned in a dungeon for a long time. Then King Zedekiah sent for him to find a word from the Lord again. This time the message was the same, "You will be given over to the Babylonians." The king was furious and had him placed in the courtyard of the guard.

He had told the people, that if they stayed in the city, they would die by the sword, famine, or the plague. The officials put him down by ropes into the muddy cistern in the courtyard of the guard and left him to die.

A compassionate guard reported this to the king and he ordered that he be lifted out of the cistern, but he stayed in the courtyard. Once again the king consulted Jeremiah, the prophet about his future. This time it was in secret and he asked again, the same question. The Babylonians were near and he wanted to know what chance he had for survival when they attacked the city of Jerusalem.

Jeremiah told him what the Lord had said. If Zedekiah surrendered all would be well. If he did not surrender he would be captured by the king of Babylon and the city would be burned.

In the ninth year of King Zedekiah, Nebuchadnezzar, King of Babylon brought his whole army against Jerusalem in Judah. In the eleventh year of King Zedekiah, the walls of Jerusalem crumbled under the onslaught of the weapons of Babylon. All the Most High officials of their enemy sat in the middle gate. Zedekiah, king of Judah, fled the city with his soldiers in the night. He was pursued and taken prisoner. All his nobles were killed, his sons were slain before his eyes, his own eyes were gouged out and he was taken to Babylon in shackles. The Babylonians laid waste the city of Jerusalem with fire. They took the people into exile in Babylon, but left the poor, the land and vineyards.

They freed Jeremiah, the prophet and asked him if he would like to go with them or stay with his people left in Judah. He chose to stay. Gedaliah was appointed governor, to rule over Judah by the king of Babylon. He was only there two months and a band of robbers came and killed him and his friends and took over.

The Jews asked Jeremiah what they should do and Jeremiah gave them God's message. He told them to stay and not be afraid of the Babylonians, because he would take care of them that they might prosper on the land once more They were adamant in their decision to go down to Egypt for safety and Jeremiah, the prophet of God followed them explaining the horrors they would suffer when Nebuchadnezzar conquered Egypt. They would all die.

Jeremiah also prophesied against God's enemies: the Philistines, the Moabites, Edom and Babylon. Tradition says he was stoned to death in Egypt. Another theory is that when the king of Babylon took Egypt, he saved him and brought him to Babylon.

PART 19

Ezekial, Prophet and Priest in Captivity

He was captured eleven years before the fall of Jerusalem and taken to Babylon, where Israel was already living. He dwelled on the banks of the river Kabar, in his own house with his wife who later died. Israel was still Godless and angry and malicious, against the God who had sent them there. He did not get a warm reception. God had told him these stiff necked, rebellious fools, would be dangerous, but he was not to fear, because God would be with him and protect him.

God appeared to him in visions and spoke to him, calling him to be a prophet to Israel as well as priest. The only hope for this remnant of God's people would be repentance and submission to their creator. He had to make them understand that their captivity was their own doing. They had been warned by the Lord what evil behavior would bring disaster down on their own heads. They knew what would happen if they did not repent of their heathen ways. God had destroyed other nations for the same activity and could have destroyed them. They needed to realize that God was giving them a second chance.

Ezekiel led them and warned them for twenty two years and earned the respect of the elders, who came to him in all situations. He was a brilliant man, well educated in international affairs and cultural differences. He was a messenger of comfort and hope as he taught them that the future would see them back in their homeland and a messiah would come someday to redeem them and reign over them in peace and harmony for a thousand years.

"You will know that I am the Lord," appears thirty times in this book. He prophesied the destruction of Jerusalem and Judah and when it was done the people began to believe. He wooed them with stories of the restoration of the temple, painting vivid pictures in their minds of future glory under the Lord's favor. He also preached and prophesied against the countries round about, who were enemies of God, and would suffer retribution under his hands.

They learned again how to worship and celebrate the festivals and feasts. They had to learn again about the temple and their duties there and renounce all foreign God's. They would have to repent and learn about the covenants and how important it was to follow God's plan and God's man.

PART 20

Daniel, Prophet of Revelation

Daniel was taken to Babylon as a young boy of noble birth with three other boys, to serve in the king's court. They were chosen because of their physical stamina and their ability to learn quickly. They were to be taught the language and the history of Babylon and educated in all the things necessary to make them ready for service to the king, Nebuchadnezzar.

They were to eat the rich food and wine from the king's table and Daniel refused. He explained to his guardian that simpler fare would make him healthier and stronger. He was allowed to test his theory and was proven right. In the next three years, he became known as an interpreter of dreams. Arioch, the king's man sent for him when he had a dream that troubled him. Daniel was called to explain it to him.

At first, Nebuchadnezzar called in all the wise men of Babylon and told them about the dream and asked them to tell him the dream and then interpret it. They were dumbfounded by such a request. They explained that it was impossible. It had never been done. He must tell them the dream first and then they could tell him its meaning. The king became furious with them and had ordered them all killed for their impertinence.

Daniel came and calmed him, after God had given him the answers in the night. The king had a vision of a huge statue, with a head of gold, chest and arms of silver, belly and thighs of bronze, and legs of iron. Its feet were partly of iron and partly of clay. While the king was watching, (but no one else was there. A rock was cut out and thrown at the statue and smashed the feet. The whole statue crumbled to the ground. The wind blew it away and the rock became a mountain and filled the whole earth.

This is the interpretation. Nebuchadnezzar is king of kings. He rules over all men and all things, because God has allowed it. He is the head of gold. After him will be another kingdom, not so successful. The third king will rule all the earth. He is bronze. The fourth kingdom will be iron, strong enough to smash everything. It will crush all the others. The feet are a divided kingdom where disunity brings them defeat. At last, God will bring a kingdom that will never be defeated and last forever. This is the future.

The king was so overjoyed to know the meaning of his dream that he praised the god of Israel, gave Daniel gifts and made him ruler over the province of Babylon and all his wise men. At Daniel's request, he also made his friends, Shadrach, Meshach, and Abednego administrators of the province so he could stay at court.

King Nebuchadnezzar made a golden statue ninety feet high and nine feet wide and had it set up on a plain in Dura in Babylon. He commanded all the officials of all the nations that he ruled to come and bow down to the statue every time the music played, and worship it. If anyone refused to do so, would be thrown into a fiery furnace.

Later, his astrologers reported that the Jewish boys did not worship the gods of Babylon or the statue. He called the boys into his presence and asked them to worship the statue and they refused. They told him that they trusted their God to save them. The king was furious and ordered the furnace to be seven times hotter than usual and had them tied up and thrown into it. The king was watching through the hole in the front, to see them burn, but they didn't. He jumped back in fear, when he saw them free from their ropes and walking around. Worse still was a figure with them. The furnace was so hot that it had burned the soldiers that threw them in and it was impossible for anyone to survive, but they did. Worse, still, the figure with them looked like a son of the gods.

He had to recognize the power of the Most High God and he called them out. They were fine, for they had not been affected by the fire at all. The king was so overwhelmed by the power of their God that he commanded that anyone who spoke a word against him would be killed and all his possessions destroyed. The Hebrew boys got promotions.

Again, the king had a fearful dream and called together all his wise men and magicians, but they could not explain its meaning. Then came Daniel to the rescue once more. The king had seen an enormous tree that had kept growing until it touched the sky. It could be seen all over the world and had an abundance of fruit and beautiful leaves. The animals and birds used it for shelter and food. Then a messenger came from the sky and shouted for him to destroy the tree and all its contents; leaves and fruit, except for the stump. It was to be wrapped in iron and bronze. The king was to be soaked with dew and live with the animals in the fields. Let his mind be like theirs until seven times have passed. The holy ones have given the sentence of the Most High God. Unless King Nebuchadnezzar renounced all his gods and stopped oppressing people, he would lose his mind and be like an animal and live with them. He would be set free when he was ready to worship only the one true God and then his kingdom would be restored.

The king disregarded the message. It was business as usual. A year later he was walking on the roof of the palace looking out over the city and reminding himself of his great ability to conquer nations and gather so much wealth. In a moment a voice from heaven condemned him for his arrogance, for it was by permission of the Most High God that he had been so fortunate. The curse from the dream took effect immediately and he was driven out into the field to dwell with the wild animals. He was there until his hair grew like the feathers of a great bird and his nails were like claws. Then, he came back to himself. His sanity had returned and he was praising and glorifying God. His kingdom was returned to him in great joy.

The next king we meet is Belshazzar, a son of Nebuchadnezzar, who was giving a banquet for a thousand of his nobles. They were all drinking wine when the king ordered the golden goblets his father had brought from the temple in Jerusalem, to drink from. While doing so, they were praising their pagan gods. Suddenly, there was a moving hand writing a message across the wall. The king was so shocked that he collapsed and called for his astrologers and magicians to come and tell him what it meant. Whoever was able to explain it would be made third in the kingdom. The wise men of his kingdom were baffled and the king was beside himself, with fear.

The queen reminded him of the man who had interpreted his father's dreams and suggested that he should call on him in his dilemma. His name was Daniel. When Daniel came, he reminded the king of what his father suffered at the hand of the one true God when he mocked him. Now the son was doing the same by drinking wine from the sacred goblets from God's house. This is God's message for him:

"God has numbered the days of your reign, and it has come to an end. You have been weighed on the scales and found wanting. Your kingdom is divided and given to the Medes and the Persians." He rewarded Daniel. And that night Belshazzar was killed and his kingdom was taken by Darius, the Mede.

Under Darius, Daniel was made an administrator and won the king's favor by his expert handling of the position, in service to his sovereign. The king decided to put him in charge of the whole kingdom. His officials were jealous of Daniel, a foreigner, to be put in such a place. They plotted to find a way to get rid of him. Because his behavior was so flawless, they could find no fault in him so they had to use his God against him. They went to the king and asked him to write an edict to throw to the lions anyone praying to anything or anyone other than the king. They got their wish.

Every day, three times, Daniel would go to his room and kneel under a window that looked in the direction of Jerusalem and prayed to God for help and these men knew that. They came and caught him praying and hauled him off to the king. The Medes and Persians had a law that a king's edict was law and could not be changed. Daniel had to be thrown into the lion's den.

When they appeared before Darius the Mede, with Daniel, The king was distraught and tried his best to find a way to save him. There was no way he could prevent it. He told Daniel that he hoped that Daniel's God could save him. The king tossed and turned all night in despair over this situation. In the morning, he went immediately to the lion's den to see if Daniel lived or died. He called out his name and Daniel answered. God had shut the lion's mouths and he was untouched. The king ordered him to be released. The officials who caused this to happen were put in the lion's den and nothing was left but bones. The king sent out a decree to all nations under his power, to worship the God of Daniel, because he was far more powerful than all the others.

Daniel was given dreams and visions of four beasts and wrote down what had occurred. God told him to seal it and keep it secret for a future time. It will be explained later in the book of Revelation. Even Daniel couldn't understand and it left him ill for several days.

Daniel read in Jeremiah 25:11-12, that the desolation of Jerusalem would last for seventy years. He was devastated by this and prayed for his people in their distress. As time passed he had more visions of the future: wars, kings, hope and desperation all to purge God's people from their wicked ways. The end time things are also revealed to Daniel. He bore a heavy burden for Israel for all his days.

PART 21

Joel, Priest and Prophet in Judah

The land has been ravaged by swarms of locusts greater than they have ever seen before. All plant life is stripped of any value and they are facing famine throughout Judah. "The storehouses are in ruin. The granaries are broken down and there is no pasture." Like the prophets in Israel, Joel is lamenting the sins of his people, who have ignored their God's commands and they deserve their fate. They must come to him in repentance and call upon him to renew their relationship with the one who controls all things. God works in mysterious ways to get man's attention. When his people sin and do not yield to the prophet's warnings, he takes radical measures; such as defeat in battle, pestilence, plagues of all kinds, even disease and death. Even so, it seems that they never learn from their history. God never changes. His commandments are written in stone!

When they return to him, he promises the great "Day of the Lord." A time will come when all their enemies will be held accountable, for what they have done to God's people. Empires will fall, but God's people will prosper. There is always hope in the Lord.

PART 22

Jonah The prophet That Said No

He was from the tribe of Zebulun. God sent him to convert pagan nations. But, when he was sent to the wicked city of Nineveh, he was adamant that these people were so evil, with all their violence, corruption, and even witchcraft, that they did not deserve God's offer of repentance. It was the capital of the Assyrian Empire, spectacular in its beauty, with many fine buildings and palaces where people lived in luxury they did not deserve. He was so distraught over this assignment that he tried to run away from God.

He got on a boat that was going in the other direction. Of course, God knew what he was doing, and raised up a storm to threaten disaster for the ship. The captain cast lots to find out who was responsible for this calamity. Of course, the lot fell to Jonah. The Lord had everything under control. They already knew that he was running away from God. They were afraid of the power of his God, so they had no idea what to do about the situation. They asked Jonah what could be done. He told them to throw him overboard, and trembling in fear they finally did. The sea was suddenly calm.

Jonah disappeared into the belly of a great fish. He lived there for three days and then was thrown onto dry land in the fishes vomit. He had prayed while he was inside the fish. When he realized where he was, he cried out to the Lord for forgiveness and promised to fulfill his mission.

God's message to this great city was this, 'In forty more days the city will be overturned." The inhabitants of Nineveh believed God and the king declared a fast. Everybody from him on down was to put on sackcloth and cry out to God for mercy. When they had repented from their evil ways, God forgave them and lifted his curse.

This is a reprieve for a gentile (not Jewish) nation, when we do not expect God to extend mercy to his enemies. He has said that he will give mercy as he chooses and in this case he knew that they would turn to him, when they were forced to realize that he was more powerful than their gods.

Jonah was beside himself with anger. He did not trust these people. He went to a place in the city where he could hide out and keep an eye on them. He had even asked God to take his life. God set about to teach him a lesson. A vine grew up over Jonah to give him shade. The next morning God had a worm eat it for breakfast. The sun blazed and the wind burned his flesh. Again he whimpered to God to let him die. God reminded him that he had nothing to do with the vine, but it grew and protected him for one day. God said, "You have been concerned about this vine, though you did not tend it or make it grow. It sprang up overnight and died overnight. But Nineveh has a hundred and twenty thousand people who do not know their right hand from their left and many cattle as well. Should I not be concerned about that great city?"

PART 23

Nahum, Prophet of Nineveh's Demise

The Assyrian capital was the scene of Jonah's success in turning the city toward God. Under another king they went back to their evil ways. They destroyed Samaria and captured Israel and took them into captivity. They were beyond cruel, they were like animals torturing their prey. They uprooted people groups and planted them in another part of their empire.

Only God has universal sovereignty. Beware the wrath of the holy one of Israel. There came the whirlwind, storm, and earthquake. The sea and all the rivers disappeared. The mountains shook. The hills melted and the earth trembled. Rocks shattered and it became a city of blood. Only those who trusted God were safe.

She was pillaged, plundered, and stripped. Hearts melted, knees gave way, bodies trembled and every face grew pale. (2:10) Her great men were put in chains.

Nineveh was located on the east bank of the Tigris River, opposite the city of Mosul. As the prophets said, it would never rise again. For centuries it was thought to be a myth, until archeologists discovered it and began excavating in the nineteenth century.

PART 24

The Time, Between the Testaments From the destruction of Jerusalem, to the birth of Jesus

When the Holy City was destroyed, the temple was gone and God was gone and the priests were gone. All the elements of the Jews religion had disappeared. The population was gone, except for the poorest who were left to tend the fields and the vineyards. They turned to the gods of their neighbors. Many of the exiles fell into step with their captors. Only when Ezra returned with the exiles from Persia, was the priest able to start a restoration of the temple. It was always the center of their religion and it beckoned to those who had been influenced by Ezra in captivity. More would add to their presence when Nehemiah came back to build the wall, and other exiles returned from Babylon. They brought back the lifestyle, the prophets and the traditions that made it their home.

When their neighbors tried to stop them from rebuilding the city, God was their helper. The Persian King made the Jewish law equal with his own as a buffer on the border of Egypt.

In 332 Alexander the great took over. Most of his conquests were easy because of his reputation. People would open the gates and welcome him so he wouldn't destroy the city. When he conquered the Persian, he left Jerusalem and Judea as it had been under the Persians. He died 323 and his holdings went to his commanders. They introduced the Greek culture, which was called Hellenism. The Jews had to learn the language in order to survive, for all business was carried out in Greek. Under this new leadership, the country changed hands frequently and the population suffered greatly.

In 301 Ptolemy who ruled Egypt ruled them and held it till 200. In the third century they fought with the Seleucids in Syria until a new king came to the throne and tried to conquer them. He didn't succeed, so he came back full force later and was defeated by the Seleucids. The Ptolemies ruled longer than anyone else.

At that time, Israel was part of the territory known as Syria and Phoenicia, without permanent borders that shifted between nations. Changes that occurred were; mixed nationalities, military colonies, and ancient cities becoming Greek. Phoenicians became bearers of Hellenism in Israel. The Jewish traditions were still being pursued in the interior. Macedonia was the exception. She had embraced the new order already.

The Seleucids held Judea. Jerusalem was ruled by the high priest and council of elders. A Jewish form of government prevailed. The Seleucids were going broke and made a treaty with the Romans to keep peace. They taxed the people beyond reason to pay the Roman tribute, beginning a break with the Jews.

When Antiochus IV Epiphanes took the throne, things changed for the Jews. For his first seven years, he focused on Egypt. From the beginning of his rule, he meddled in the affairs of Jerusalem. He deposed the high priest and replaced him with his own brother,

Jason. He leaned toward Hellenism and vowed to collect more taxes than those before him. He also changed the administration of Jerusalem, making it a Polis (Greek city state).

In 171, Menelaus took over. The king, with his help, took the temple treasures to help pay for his war on Egypt. A year later, the king was reported killed in battle. His brother Jason took the city. First he punished the citizens. He brought a group of his own people to run everything and Jews were pushed aside. The Sabbath and circumcision were banned on penalty of death.

In 167 the temple was dedicated to the Greek god Zeus. The Jews, so devoted to their God and their way of life didn't give up any of it. Martyrdom became the order of the day and they began to believe that their suffering would bring the end of days.

Rising against these atrocities in this era was the Hasmonean dynasty (priests from Modi in Lydia). They led a revolt. For about 130 years, the Jews depended on them. Mattathias led the rebels in guerilla warfare. He was drawing together large groups to fight the army. They fought from town to village and eventually had Jerusalem cut off from Seleucid power.

When he died, his sons took over. Judas Maccabee was famous for his military prowess had four victories over the enemy army. He liberated Jerusalem and cleansed the temple and brought priests to tend it. To celebrate this accomplishment a festival called Hannukah was instituted. It has continued to be celebrated down through the generations.

The king finally executed Menelaus for his policies that they blamed for the rebellion. They tried to get things back under control, by giving the Jews religious freedom. A new king took the throne in

Syria in162 and was defeated by Judah Maccabee. He made a treaty with Rome. He died in battle in 160.

His brothers restarted the guerilla warfare. When Alexander the great came on the scene, he made them high priests. They held that office for a hundred years. Many cities came under their rule. The army of the Jews grew strong in Judea. By the twenties, they gained independence and all the land of Israel.

Independence ended when the Roman commander Pompey took three months to gain control of Jerusalem in 63. Thousands were killed. Syria became a Roman province and Judea became dependent on Rome.

Later Julius Caesar regarded the Jews as allies. The walls of Jerusalem were rebuilt once again. In 37 Jerusalem fell to the Romans and Herod ruled in Jerusalem and Judea.

An introduction to the New Testament

The Old Testament is all but ignored by most people, even pastors. Some think it is only a myth passed down through the ages or just a history of the Jews. They are sadly mistaken. If you have read the Bible from Genesis to Revelation, you get the big picture. It is the history of the human race from the beginning of creation to the hereafter. You will see the Old testament quoted by the Apostles and by Christ, himself. It was their Bible. It had not been put together like the book we hold in our hands, but on scrolls and passed from church to church and copied by scribes who did nothing else for their occupation. The prophets and even kings read them aloud to the people who gathered on special Holy Days. These that we have just met in the first part of this book are our ancestors and the ancestors of our Lord, Jesus Christ.

In the next pages you will see the continuity of our story. Jesus, the Christ of God, is the Messiah that the prophets talked about. The savior that was coming to save them from extinction, from the line of King David. The sad thing is, that they are still waiting. They wanted a Messiah that would lead them to victory over all their enemies and establish Jerusalem as his capital. They didn't recognize the baby in the manger as any such thing. Isaac (Israel) and Ishmael (Muslims) are still fighting each other and there is no peace.

What we find in the New Testament is the way of peace. Amidst the anxiety, chaos and confusion of this modern world, there is no peace. Jesus came to be our peace. The God of hope is still in business and a savior was born to show us the way.

MATTHEW

Matthew was a tax collector in Capernaum, a prosperous fishing area governed by the Romans. Tax collectors were hated, because they could charge anything they wanted as long as Rome got its payment. His booth was located near the Roman garrison. Capernaum was also the headquarters of Jesus ministry.

Matthew's book is a life of Christ as it affected converted Jews. Jesus met him at his workplace and called him to follow him. He gave a great feast at his home to honor the lord and promised to pay back more than he got, if he had cheated anybody. He became one of the twelve. He was in the upper room at the last supper. Tradition tells us that he preached in Judea, after Jesus ascension for twelve to fifteen years and then went to other nations.

Matthew presents Jesus as the promised king from David's line, who would be our Messiah. He gives us the life of Jesus: his birth, his ministry, his crucifixion and his glorious resurrection. This is why many consider this book the most important one in the New Testament. It is a biography of our savior and an evangelical movement to prove to the Jews that he is who he claims to be. He uses scripture to prove his case and quotes the Old Testament more than any other writer.

First he gives the genealogy Of Jesus, Beginning with Abraham and ending with Joseph, the husband of Mary, the mother of Jesus who is called the Christ. According to the Jews, Joseph was his legal father, but Matthew knew he was not his biological parent. You may also note that Joseph was from the line of David.

Mary was betrothed to Joseph. It was like our engagement except it was so committed that you would have to get divorced to break it. There could be no sexual contact until the marriage ceremony and the bed would be checked for blood in the morning to prove she was a virgin. If she was not a virgin, she could have been publicly stoned.

Mary became pregnant by the will of God, through the Holy Spirit before they came together. She knew that she had been chosen to birth God's son, because she was visited by an angel who had explained what was going to happen to her. Joseph did not understand at first, until an angel came to him and let him know that he should marry her, because she had been chosen by God for this special purpose and was still innocent.

Matthew 1:17 Thus there were fourteen generations in all from Abraham to David, fourteen from David to the exile to Babylon and fourteen from the exile to the Christ.

Verse 21 She will give birth to a son and you are to give him the name Jesus, because he will save his people from sin. Verse 23 The virgin will be with child and will give birth to a son and they will call him Immanuel, which means, "God with us."

When Jesus was born in Bethlehem, the Magi, wise men from Persia, came to Jerusalem to ask the king where to find him. They believed the prophets who told of a sign in the sky that pointed the way. They had been following the star for a long time. Herod was upset when they asked him for directions to the new king of the

Jews. He asked his wise men where this king was to be born. They told him, Bethlehem in Judea, the city of David. He sent them on their way with directions for them to stop on their way back and tell him where he was found.

By this time, they no longer lived in the stable, but in a house, and the star appeared above it to guide them. They worshiped him and gave him gifts of gold, frankincense (incense) and myrrh (perfume). While there, they had a dream, telling them not to go back to the king, so they went home another way.

Herod was so angry when they didn't come back, that he gave an order that all Jewish baby boys were to be thrown in the river and this is what was happening when we learned of the saving of Moses' life in Egypt.

An angel told Joseph to take his family to Egypt and stay there until it was safe to come back. When Herod died he was told that he could go back. When he came near, he found out that Herod's son had taken the throne, he went to the town of Nazareth. The prophets had said, "He will be called a Nazarene."

JOHN THE BAPTIST

When Mary was pregnant, she paid a visit to her cousin, Elizabeth who was also expecting a few months sooner than Mary. When Mary grew close, the baby leaped in Elizabeth's womb as if in greeting. Her son John was chosen by God to be the messenger to the people that the Christ would come to save Israel. He preached in the desert and baptized believers for repentance of sin.

God had told John how to recognize his son, who would come to him for baptism.

"A voice of one calling in the desert, prepare ye the way of the Lord. Make straight paths for him." (Isaiah 40:3)

The Pharisees and the Sadducees came to check him out and he warned them to repent and be baptized with water. They would need to be ready for the one who was coming, more powerful than he. He told them that the next one would baptize with fire and the Holy Spirit.

Jesus came to John for baptism and John knew who he was. He was hesitating to baptize him saying, Jesus should baptize him. Jesus convinced him that it had to be done. At the moment he came up out of the water, heaven opened and God's spirit, like a dove, came down and lighted on him. A Voice from heaven spoke, "This is my son, whom I love. With him I am well pleased."

'Jesus went into the desert to be tempted." After fasting for forty days and nights, the devil came to do his worst. He knew the Lord was hungry and asked him to prove he was the son of God, by turning stones to bread. Jesus' answer was, "It is written: "Man does not live by bread alone, but on every word that comes from the mouth of God." Next, he took Jesus to the highest point of the temple and told him to prove himself by jumping, for it was written that no harm could come to him. Jesus answered and said, "It is also written, do not put God to the test." Then he took him to a high mountain and offered to give him all the kingdoms of the word, if he would bow down and worship him. Jesus answer was, "Away from me Satan, for it is written; 'Worship the Lord your God, and serve him only." That ended that encounter and angels came to meet his needs.

While he was away preaching, the lord heard that John had been imprisoned. Scenting danger he moved to Capernaum, which became his place of refuge, fulfilling another prophecy of Isaiah.

(Isaiah 9:2). John was beheaded by Herod for pointing out his sin with his brother's wife.

APOSTLES CHOSEN

Walking by the sea of Galilee Jesus came upon the brothers; Simon Peter and Andrew. They were fisherman. He stopped and said," Come follow me," and they did. James and John, their partners, followed also. They left everything and it was a profitable business. Andrew and Simon Peter were disciples of John the Baptist. One day, Andrew was with him and John pointed out Jesus and called him the "Lamb of God." He rushed to where Peter was and said, "We have found the Messiah!" They ran to meet him and when they found him, he greeted Simon Peter, "You are Simon, son of John. You shall be called Cephas." (Peter) (John 1:36-42). They went back to work until John the Baptist was put in prison. Then Jesus came and told them to follow him.

Jesus called the four partners at the same time, by coming into their boat and asking them to head out a ways so he could speak to the crowd that was following him everywhere he went. When they were fishing they were not having a good day. They had fished all night and not caught any fish. Jesus told them to go out into deeper water and throw out their nets and they came back full, all the boat would hold. (Luke 5:1-7)

Later Jesus healed Peter's mother-in- law. Peter followed Jesus to Galilee, Decapolis, Perea, and Judea. He was with him when he raised Jairus' daughter. He walked on the sea. In the middle of a windy night, they saw what they thought was a ghost, walking toward them on the water and they were scared to death. He spoke to them and told them not to be afraid and they recognized his voice. Peter called out to make sure he was the Lord and asked him to let him walk on the water, and he did. Peter started to walk toward him for a little way and then took his eyes off Jesus and sank. Jesus took him by the hand and led him back to the ship.

Peter, James and John were with Jesus on the Mount of transfiguration. Peter was there when Jesus explained the mystery of the fig tree. A time came when Jesus asked the twelve, "Who do you say that I am?" Peter's answer was, "You are the Christ, the son of the living God."

At the last supper, Jesus was washing their feet and Peter refused because he thought he didn't deserve it, but Jesus told him he would have no part in him if he didn't. When Jesus was put on trial, Peter was outside with a crowd around him, when he was accused of being one of his followers. He denied that he even knew him. In fact, he denied him three times just as Jesus had said he would, after he promised forever loyalty.

At Gethsemane, when Jesus was being arrested, Peter took his sword and sliced off the ear of the High Priest's servant. The Lord rebuked him and healed the ear. Peter was fist Apostle to enter the empty tomb.

The third time he appeared to his disciples after the resurrection, he reinstated a repentant Peter. He told him to feed his lambs and take care of the sheep. He commanded him," Feed my sheep. I tell you the truth, when you were younger, you dressed yourself and went where you wanted; but when you are old, you will stretch out your hands, and someone else will dress you and lead you where you do not want to go." This was a warning, for he would be crucified on a cross, upside down at his own request.

Peter was afterward considered their leader even though he did not impose himself in any way into their business. He got them to replace Judas who gave up Christ to the enemy and died for it afterwards. He preached a miraculous sermon at Pentecost, when three thousand people were saved. He told a beggar that he had nothing else to give him. He told him to get up and walk and he did. He was imprisoned for preaching in Acts 3. An angel let him out. In Samaria he rebuked a sorcerer.

Three years later he met Paul. He visited churches. Then James, the brother of John, and the youngest of the twelve was the first one to be martyred. He was killed by Herod. He then took Peter prisoner under four squads of soldiers and this was when the angel set him free. Years later he appeared in Jerusalem, at a conference on circumcising converts. The answer was, no need. Jesus was enough, even for the Gentile believers. Peter, James and John were his inner circle. Peter was a joint founder of the Roman church. He and Paul were killed at about the same time, under Nero.

Andrew pointed out the boy with the loaves and fishes, when Jesus fed the five thousand. He was in the upper room. He preached in various places until he was crucified on an x cross, tied with cords to make him suffer longer in Achaia, for refusing to worship foreign Gods.

John was also a disciple of John the Baptist. He and his brother James were the sons of Zebedee, a prosperous fisherman. In his writings; the gospel of John, and his letters, and the book of Revelation. He refers to himself as "the other disciple'" or "the one whom Jesus loved." They were closer than brothers all through Jesus ministry. John was the only apostle at the cross, with Jesus' mother and the other women. He was fearless in his faith, while the others were hiding out in the upper room. He was beside the Lord in almost every point of his ministry. Jesus called John and James, "Sons of thunder."

He was at the healing of Peter's mother-in-law, the ordination of the apostles, at the raising of Jairus' daughter, and on the Mount of

Olives, with Jesus foretelling the destruction of Jerusalem. At the time of the Lord's betrayal, he and Peter followed at a distance to the palace of Caiaphas, where Jesus was taken. Because John was an acquaintance, he was allowed in. From the cross, the Lord told him to take care of his mother. Peter and John were at the tomb and also at the ascension. He and Peter both preached to the Samaritans. Fifteen years after Paul' first visit, he was still in Jerusalem, a pillar of the church. He settled a conflict between the Jews and gentiles. In the book of Revelation {1:9) we learn of his exile to the Island of Patmos and a visitation from the Lord, who directed him in writing letters to seven churches in which their worthiness was revealed. Tradition says that he was shipwrecked off the coast of Ephesus. He was boiled in oil by Domitian, and was not injured.

He wrote his gospel in Ephesus. He taught the Jews to celebrate Easter. He lived to be very old and was highly respected. He was taken to meeting on a stretcher and his final words to them were, "Little children, love one another."

Matthew, in chapters five through seven gives us the content of Jesus' Sermon on the Mount. It begins with what are called the Beatitudes, where he lists all those God calls blessed. Then he explains salt and light. In him, we are the salt of the earth, in God's favor, walking in the light of Jesus and reflecting who he is to those around us. We have to choose to follow him. Just as salt has to be kept from losing its flavor, we can also be polluted by the world.

Jesus explains that he has not come to eliminate the law and the prophets, but he has come to fulfill them. He also tells us how to live peacefully and please God with our choices. He emphasizes some of the commandments. We are to bear good fruit. For the wicked, when they come to the judgment, they will hear these words, "Sorry, I never knew you."

He healed the lepers, and brought faith to a centurion. When he healed Peter's mother-in-law, all the sick from miles around came to him and he healed them all, no matter what the problem was. He even healed the demon possessed. He taught the people about fasting.

He used parables to help people understand what he was teaching them. He used examples from everyday life. An example: In the parable of the lost sheep, Jesus tells of a shepherd who has a hundred sheep and one is lost. He leaves the ninety nine to go and find the lost sheep. This is the way God loves his own and would not have even one to perish.

Then Jesus preached in his home town, even his own family did not accept him as a prophet. "After all, isn't this the carpenter's son?" Jesus said, "Only in his hometown, and in his own house is a prophet without honor."

Herod was not the only one who was out to get him. The Pharisee resented his leading people away from their authority. They were always trying to find some fault in what he said or did, so they could persecute him. They served under the Romans, so they could not harm him without their permission and only the Romans could take a life.

Jesus went up on a mountain and sat down, as the crowds brought him their sick and disabled loved ones for healing. "The people were amazed when they saw the mute speaking, the crippled made well, the lame walking and the blind seeing. And they praised the God of Israel." (Matthew 15:31) Then he fed the whole assembly with seven loaves and a few small fish for four thousand people. In another place he had fed five thousand people with five loaves and two fish and had leftovers. (Matthew 16:9-10)

Later Jesus predicted his own death. He would suffer many things at the hands of "the elders, chief priests and teachers of the law." He would be killed and then rise on the third day.

Peter protested and Jesus revealed, this was a message from Satan and rebuked him. Six days later, he took Peter, James and John up a high mountain that we refer to as the Mount of Transfiguration, where he was changed right before their eyes. "His face shone like the sun, and his clothes became as white as the light. Just then there appeared before them Moses and Elijah talking to Jesus." A voice from Heaven spoke from a cloud and said, "This is my son whom I love; with him I am well pleased. Listen to him."

The Pharisees asked, "Is it lawful for a man to divorce his wife any and every reason." Jesus answered and said that when one marries, the two become one flesh and "What God has joined together, let no man separate." Adultery is the only excuse and if you can't find a keeper, stay single.

We never hear of domestic violence in the Bible. We do hear of men marrying a wife for purposes of heirs and household reasons, men who have other women on the side as well. They worship other gods for the most part unless they are kings, who go against God's laws. In our day, if you have been divorced before you accepted Jesus as your savior, all your sins have been forgiven that happened before. Someone addicted to pornography could be called an adulterer. "The lust of the eyes." (1 John 2:16) Each case is to be decided with a merciful God who protects the innocent.

Jesus blessed the little children. "Let the little children come to me and do not hinder them, for the kingdom of heaven belongs to such as these" (Matthew 19:14).

Jesus speaks of his death again as he and his disciples are on the road to Jerusalem. The time has come for him to fulfill the prophecies of his death and resurrection. As they near the city, he sends them to get a donkey for him to ride and tells them exactly where to find it and what to tell the owner.

His ride into the city is what we celebrate as Palm Sunday or the Triumphal Entry. Crowds went ahead and behind as people spread Palms in the road before him to keep down the dust. They were shouting praises to God.

Jesus went straight to the temple and drove out the buyers and sellers who were doing business there. "My house will be a house of prayer, but you are making it a den of robbers." (Matthew 21:13) Jesus preached in the temple. The priests and the Pharisees were afraid to arrest him because the crowd believed he was a prophet. They made another plan to trap him.

They asked him if it was right or wrong to pay taxes to Caesar. Jesus asked for a coin and held it up. He wanted to know whose picture and inscription was on it. Of course, it was Caesar's. His answer was, "Give to Caesar that which is Caesar's and to God what is God's." (Matthew 22:21)

He talked about the arrogance of the Pharisees and he pronounced seven woes on the Jewish authorities. As he left the temple he cited some of the signs to watch for at the end of the age. In chapter twenty one. No one knows the day or the hour when he will come again. God does not set dates. He acts in the fullness of time. As with Nineveh in the time of Jonah; God allowed a second chance. They obeyed and saved their city. For years to come until the fullness of time when there was no more hope. Then he destroyed it.

It was time for the Passover feast; the time for him to be taken and crucified. The high priest Caiaphas and his henchmen were plotting in his house to find a way to make it happen. It would have to be after the Passover, so the crowds would be gone.

Jesus was visiting some people in Bethany, when a woman with "a very expensive jar of perfume," came in and poured it over his head. The disciples were disgusted with such waste. It could have been sold and the money given to the poor. Jesus stunned them when he said that she was preparing him for burial. They still hadn't faced the fact that it was really going to happen. Jesus said that people will always remember what she did.

Judas Iscariot, one of the twelve who had dipped his hand in their treasury and helped himself, went and made a deal with the enemy, for thirty pieces of silver, and planned to give them their wish. He was a zealot, ready to fight a physical battle and found Jesus too meek and mild for his liking.

The time for the Passover meal was at hand; what we call the lords Supper. It took place in a private home, so they would have privacy. During the meal, Jesus announced that one of them would betray him. When Judas asked, "Is it I?" Jesus replied, "It is you." Then he performed the first communion service. He gave the wine to represent his blood and the bread to represent his body. He asked them to do this in remembrance of him after he was gone. When they had finished, they went to the Mount of Olives.

Jesus went off by himself to pray and the others went to sleep. Alone in the agony of what was to come, he sweat drops of blood and they were not paying attention. He went back to where they were and found all of them still asleep. Judas was coming with a crowd of armed men. He came near and kissed Jesus on the cheek so they would know which one to take. Jesus was ready to go willing when

Peter took a sword and lopped off the ear of a servant. Jesus rebuked him and put it back on. The Lord was arrested and taken away to the High priest. He was ready to do what he was born for; to die for the sins of mankind, so we could be reconciled to God the father.

Before the Jewish court the High priest charged him with claiming that he was the Christ, the son of God. Jesus said, "Yes, it is as you say. But I say to all of you, in the future you will see the son of man sitting at the right hand of the Mighty One and coming on the clouds of heaven. (Matthew 26:64)

They trapped him for blasphemy. Then they beat him with their fists. They decided to put him to death for claiming to be God and took him to Pilate the governor.

By this time, Judas had great remorse for what he had done to an innocent man. He tried to give back his blood money and it was refused. He took it and threw it across the floor of the temple and went away and hung himself.

Pilate was beside himself as to what to do with Jesus. He could not find any fault with him, but if he went against the Jews, there would be a riot and he would be in trouble with Rome. He brought out a hardened criminal named Barabbas and had him stand with Jesus and asked the crowd which one should be set free and the crowd roared, "Give us Barabbas." Pilate had nightmares after that.

Jesus was crucified on a hill called Golgotha, (we call Calvary) outside Jerusalem. He had to carry his own cross through the city streets. He was placed between two thieves. One mocked him and the other believed he was who he said he was. He told that one that he would be with him in paradise on the same day. The Easter story tells of his suffering for the sins of all mankind and then rising again and appearing to many, before his ascension into heaven.

Jesus had told his disciples to go to a certain mountain after his death and he met them there and gave them The Great Commission: "Go into all the world and preach my gospel," and that became their life's purpose. The hope that he had brought would not die with him, but has come down through the ages because they became missionaries to their neighbors and the nations round about them. "He came not to condemn the world," but so that we might be saved from the evil of this world. He did not come to bring peace as the Jews expected from their Messiah. He came to be our peace and he still is. Matthew gave them more hope by pointing out the prophets predictions of his second coming, to set up a new kingdom of peace in this world.

"For as the lightning comes out of the east, and shines even to the west; so shall also the coming of the son of man be." Matthew 24:27

"When the son of man shall come in his glory, and all the holy angels with him, then shall he sit upon the throne of his glory and before him shall be gathered all nations…" Matthew 25:31-32

MARK

The book of Mark is the shortest of the four gospels. He sees Jesus as servant. His mother's house was a meeting place for believers. He learned these things from listening to the preaching of Peter. Our first sight of him is when he left Jerusalem with Paul and Barnabas, when they went to Antioch, as Paul's helper. He went with them on their first missionary trip. After that he left Paul with his cousin Barnabas on less than friendly terms. Years later he had regained favor with Paul. We know no more of him except his book.

As Matthew wrote for Jewish converts, Mark is writing for Gentiles, probably at Rome. He focuses on the importance and the necessity of the cross, his service to humanity as the son of God and messiah. Jesus was born to die by crucifixion. The prophets of old spelled out the whole process of salvation from the exile from the Garden of Eden to the day it happened. Only a sinless human could pay the price for the sins of mankind, who mocked God for centuries with no repentance. By sending Jesus into the world with the message of faith and forgiveness he once again gives us a chance to inherit heaven instead of hell. Hope, once again becomes a viable commodity. The cross is a monument of God's love and compassion. The empty cross and the empty tomb prove that his work was finished here and was not finished in heaven as he is still our path to God the father by the power of the Holy Spirit that he sent to be our comforter.

LUKE

Luke was a, well educated, Greek doctor who traveled with Paul. He wrote the book that bears his name as well as the book of the Acts of the Apostles. They are both addressed to a man named Theophilus, probably an important new believer, who seems to have a lot of questions about the whole scheme of things concerning Christianity. Luke presented Jesus as a man. Jesus himself referred to himself as The Son of Man and of course he was through his mother, as well as the Son of God through his father.

At the beginning of his book he informs us that he has become a historian of sorts, because he has investigated all these things for himself and has searched out witnesses to verify the truth of the events he is reporting. He is presenting Jesus to the whole world so anyone who reads his book will know that Jesus does not play favorites, but he came and ministered and died for all. It does not matter who you are or where you came from or what you do or have done.

He tells the story of Mary meeting the angel who comes to tell her, her future as the mother of the son of God. A sweet young virgin who cannot understand why she has been chosen for such an honor.

In chapter two he tells of the savior's birth, with the star and the shepherds and the wise men, that we hear every year at Christmas.

The baby in the manger is the Christ of the cross, coming to save the world a beacon of hope in a world gone mad. On the eighth day he was presented in the temple to be consecrated to God. They were met by an old man named Simeon who had been promised through the Holy Spirit, that he would not die until he saw the Christ of God. On the day they were there, he was moved to enter the temple and was able to fulfill that prophecy, and he was able to hold the child in his arms. So too was an old woman named Anna, a prophetess. She prayed in the temple day and night and knew he was the one who would redeem Israel. In chapter 3:23 we find Jesus family tree from Mary's father Heli, back to God. She was also in the line of King David.

Luke names all twelve of the apostles: Peter, Andrew, James and John, Philip, Bartholomew, Matthew, Thomas, James son of Alpheus, Simon, who was called a zealot, Judas, son of James, and Judas Iscariot, the traitor.

Phillip was probably a friend of Andrew and Peter. He came to Jesus soon after they did. We do not know much about him. He invited Nathanial to come and see Jesus, he was at the church in Jerusalem and the ascension. He preached the gospel in Phrygia and died in Syria. In the book of Acts, Luke tells of his preaching in Samaria and miracles happening, Paralytics were healed and demons fled the scene as people were set free. Even Simon, the magician, succumbed to his preaching. Peter and John came to see them baptized with the Holy Spirit, when they heard of Philip's success. The sorcerer saw that the spirit came with the laying on of hands and offered them money to teach him how to do it. When they condemned him for such thoughts, he asked them to pray for him.

Philip had an experience with an Ethiopian. God directed him to the man who was the treasurer for his Queen. He had gone to Jerusalem to worship. He had stopped his chariot and was reading the writings of the prophet Isaiah and as Philip came near, he could see that the man was disturbed by something. He did not understand what he had been reading and needed somebody to explain it to him. As they moved along the road he explained the good news of Jesus Christ and his saving grace to fallen man. They came near some water and the man asked to be baptized and Philip assisted him. When he was finished, he was swept away and the man saw him no more. Philip was now in a place called Azontus and preached in all the towns until Caesarea.

Bartholomew is also known as Nathaneal. He is usually accompanied by Philip. He was one of those who saw Jesus after the resurrection. He was also present at Christ's ascension into heaven. He is believed to have preached in India, Arabia, and Armenia, where he was to be flayed (stripped of his skin) alive and then crucified upside down, just as Peter was. He was a peaceful soul, dedicated to his calling.

Thomas is presented by John in his gospel as the one who said they should go and die with him, when Jesus was leaving for Bethany after Lazarus died. He knew there was danger whenever he appeared in large public gatherings. When Jesus came into the upper room after the crucifixion, he was not present. When the others told him about the visit, he did not believe it. He would have to see him for himself. This is where we get our saying; a doubting Thomas. The next time he appeared to them, he told Thomas to put his fingers in the nail prints and his hand in his side where the spear had slashed his side. Thomas said, "My Lord and my God." Tradition has him preaching in Parthia and Persia. Some have him buried in Edessa and others say he was killed by a lance.

James, the son of Alpheus, also known as James the less, was the son of Mary's sister-in-law and therefore a cousin of the Lord. He was called James the less, because he was younger and shorter than James the brother of John. We have little information concerning him.

Simon the zealot; There is no pertinent information relating to this man except that he was one of the twelve.

Judas, son of James; James the less perhaps. There is no record of his activities after the resurrection.

Luke gives us this well known speech of the Lord about loving our enemies. "But, I tell you who hear me; Love your enemies, do good, to those who hate you, bless those who curse you. Pray for those who mistreat you…." He is not telling us to be door mats for others to walk on. He is using extremes to teach us to be generous to the needy. Jesus saw a funeral procession for a widow's only son. She was weeping for her loss and the fact that now she had no one to help support her. Jesus told him to get up and he did.

In chapter nine Jesus gives the twelve the power to cure people's ills and to caste out demons and sent them out to heal and to preach the kingdom of God. In chapter eleven he teaches them to pray, using what we call the Lord's Prayer which was not a prayer at all but directions on how to proceed with your own prayer. His book is filled with wonderful parables which help us to understand many things. His main theme is; repent for there is no other way to escape the punishment for your sin, because Jesus already paid for it on the cross. Chapter twenty tells of his priesthood.

After the cross, Jesus appeared to hundreds of people; some were alone and some were in large groups.

ACTS

This is an explanation of the works of the apostles and the first thirty years of the church, spanning much of the Roman Empire and includes the life of Paul that we do not get in his letters.

Luke begins this book by describing the ascension of Jesus into heaven, after he has suffered the pain of the cross and visited hundreds of people over a period of forty days, to prove that he had risen. Now, his disciples have gathered with him to watch him go to his father in heaven. He had told them to stay in Jerusalem, because in a few days they would be baptized with the Holy Spirit. He promised that the Holy Spirit would give them power to preach his gospel to the ends of the earth. They watched him being taken up above the clouds and stood there looking up for a long time. Suddenly two men in white stood before them to tell them that he would someday come back the same way.

Pentecost was upon them. They were gathered together when, suddenly like a mighty wind, the Holy Spirit came upon each one of them in tongues of fire, giving them the power to speak in other languages. A power they would need for going into all the world. This fulfilled the promise Jesus made as he prepared to leave them.

A crowd gathered around them. Each one was amazed when they heard them praising God in their own language. At the time of

Pentecost, people of many lands gathered in Jerusalem. When some of them accused the apostles of being drunk, Peter got up and quoted the Prophet Joel, who said, In the last days, God says, "I will pour out my spirit on all people..." (Joel 2:28-32)

Peter preached an overwhelming sermon, convicting them of killing the promised Messiah. But God had raised him from the dead. He told them to repent and be saved and three thousand responded on that day. Later, Peter and John were arrested for peaching the resurrection. The Sadducees had them arrested because they did not believe in the afterlife. The apostles explained, before the court, that they had used the power of God's spirit to heal a beggar and everyone in the city saw him, who was crippled, walking. They could not argue with what everybody knew of their God's power and let them go with a threat, that if they didn't stop preaching, they would face them again.

The men of God went about preaching and teaching the word of the Lord and were persecuted in many ways in many places. They were still using their power to heal and saved many.

PAUL

He was born to Jewish parents and his father was a Pharisee and from him he gained the rights of a Roman citizen. As a boy he learned a trade, and was a tent maker. He was sent to Jerusalem to study under the great teacher, Gamaliel, to learn the law.

A man of God named Stephen, did many signs and wonders in the power of God and, enemies from foreign lands came against him and brought false witnesses to court, to persecute him, and he was sentenced to be stoned. He died on his knees praising God. On the sidelines stood a young man named Saul from Tarsus, watching over the coats of those throwing stones, approving the carnage. (Later named Paul)

On that day, began a great persecution of the church at Jerusalem and the members fled the city, except for the apostles. Saul had been appointed to destroy their work and went house to house to find Christians and took them off to prison, to be tortured for their faith, thinking he was doing God a favor by getting rid of these blasphemers, both men and women. He even tried to get them to deny Christ.

Carrying out his obsession with persecuting Christians, he had papers from the High Priest to go to Damascus and bring back prisoners to Jerusalem. On the road he was stopped in his tracks. A

120

light from heaven struck him down to the ground and a voice from heaven exclaimed, "Saul, Saul, why do you persecute me?" Saul replied, "Lord, who are you?" Jesus identified himself and told him to go into the city and he would be told what to do. Paul rose to find that he was blind. He had to be led by the hand into the city and remained blind for three days and did not eat or drink anything. His companions on the road had heard the noise, but did not understand what had happened to him. Jesus called a disciple named Ananias to go and lay his hands on Saul and restore his sight' Saul was already praying and had a vision of the man coming to heal him. Ananias had heard reports of this man who had come to take prisoners of Christians, and the Lord replied, "Go! He is my chosen instrument to carry my name before the Gentiles and before their kings and before the people of Israel. I will show him how much he will suffer for my name." (Acts 9:15-16). Paul was filled with the Holy Spirit, regained his sight and was baptized.

He joined the disciples in Damascus for a few days and then began preaching Jesus in the synagogues, amazing the people who had known he was the enemy. He became more and more successful at convincing them that Jesus was the Christ. The Jews planned to kill him, but the disciples let him down over the city wall in a basket, and he went to Jerusalem. The disciples there were afraid of him till Barnabas took him to the apostles. When he was in danger they sent him home to Tarsus. Then there was a time of peace.

Paul and Barnabas were sent to Cyprus by the Jerusalem council on their first missionary journey. Later John Mark was there to help them. This is where Paul confronted a sorcerer that was struck blind and the proconsul that was present became a believer. From there they went from place to place preaching the good news of Jesus and it was in Antioch that they were first called Christians.

His second missionary journey was with Silas and he revisited the churches he had already started. He picked up Timothy and took him along. In a vision God told them to go and preach in Macedonia. Luke joined them at Troas. Converts were made, demons cast out and they were cast into prison. God rescued them with an earthquake and the jailer was converted and baptized when he found that nobody ran away, saving him from certain death. The rulers were nervous when they found out they were Roman citizens and let them go.

At Thessalonica, Paul preached Christ in the synagogue for three Sabbaths and made many converts. A riot followed and they were helped to escape. Paul sailed to Athens. In the city full of idols, he preached Christ to the Jews, telling them that their Messiah had come. He also spoke to the philosophers, who met daily in the Agora to seek knowledge. They listened to him out of curiosity. In Acts 17:22-31, he makes his case for Christ to the pagan Athenians. "He stood in the midst of Mars Hill," and pointed out that he had seen an altar to an unknown god. This is the God I serve, he told them and explained that he was the one and only God Almighty, who created all things and was above all gods, Master of the universe and mankind. Gods made by the hand of man are worthless and you must throw away your idols and worship him. He told them about Jesus who came to save them and was dead and then lived again. Some mocked him, but others believed. He reasoned in the synagogue each Sabbath until he was mistreated and then went to preach to the gentiles. His ministry is defined in the letters he wrote to his churches. Copies were made and shared with the others after they were received. We can read them in the New Testament. In fact they make up the bulk of that part of the Bible. They are: Romans, 1and 2 Corinthians, Galatians, Ephesians, Philippians, Colossians, 1 and 2 Thessalonians, 1 and 2 timothy, Titus and Philemon.

Many of them are answers to letters he received. He ministered to them wherever he was. Whether he was in prison or under house arrest in Rome, always mindful of the blessed hope he had found in Christ Jesus. He was helping them in their struggle against and God's enemies in the world. He had a painful infirmity that we cannot diagnose, but Jesus was his strength and shield.

He was given the mission to establish the church and to assure that God's purpose for mankind was not for condemnation, but for saving grace throughout the nations. It can only be found in the Lord Jesus Christ. The hope for peace in a world full of chaos and confusion had come and Paul had been sent to spread the good news.

After twenty years of service he was decapitated by the Romans and buried in the catacombs.

The book of Romans is sometimes called the constitution of Christianity. The first chapter is a must read, for it is aimed at a culture steeped in all kinds of sin very much like ours today and gives us a handle on how God will deal with it. The demise of the lost empires of history came about because of sin and sexual sin is one of the great reasons for them all to be gone. Paul warned them and died for it.

JOHN

The theme of John's book is that Jesus is God. He never left his side from the time he was called to follow him and even stood at the foot of the cross and watched him being tortured even unto death. He then took care of Mary his mother, as Jesus had asked and spent the rest of his life, writing all he knew as an eye witness to history and praising his lord even in exile on the island of Patmos. He was allowed to live to a ripe old age and die of natural causes.

In his gospel he is proving that Jesus is God and in his letters he is talking about love, family and being wary of false teachers. The book of Revelation is a revealing of what God told the prophet Daniel to hide. It is a revealing of how the world will end and what comes after.

HEBREWS

The Jews were first called by that name in Genesis 14:13. The unknown author advised the new Christians to throw away all things Jewish and abide in Christ and his teachings. He places the Lord above history and Moses and Joshua.

JAMES

This is the Brother of Jesus. He did not recognize Jesus' mission until he appeared to him after the empty tomb. There were other brothers and sisters: Joseph, Simon, Judas and all his sisters. (Matthew 13:55-56) James held an important place in the Jerusalem church and was known as "James the Just, because of his virtue." He was the head of the first church council and was a leader, well respected, among the Christians.

This was a circular letter to the twelve tribes scattered abroad from the exiles and many were very far from the Lord. He was encouraging them to Follow Jesus and to come back to their homeland. He was telling them how to find peace and rest in the Lord. There were those who had followed after foreign Gods. Some had suffered and lost everything. He tried to help them to understand that the world can be cruel if you have no one to depend on and this savior is dependable. He tried to give them hope for their future.

JUDE

Jude is another brother of the Lord who came to faith after the empty tomb. Here we find a problem that does not seem to be dealt with by others, at least with such vehemence. Jude is fighting an infestation of evil that is creeping like a plague amongst them. A creed of Gnosticism is being spread by false teachers who tell them that after you are saved, your sins do not count against you anymore. You can do what you want and it doesn't matter. They even deny Jesus Christ.

Heretics and apostasy prevail in some groups, even among their shepherds. He is admonishing the brethren to turn them to the truth and rebuke them in the name of the Lord. Those who pervert the grace of God will feel eternal fire.

REVELATION

Most people ignore the book of Revelation, because it is a complex book and there are several different opinions about what is really going on. Many books have been written trying to unravel all the numbers and the things that appear, but I am only looking for the hope it brings at the end of things. The Bible is a complete history of mankind. In the beginning and in the end it is still God that dominates. Earth and man are created and earth and man are gone. The beginning and the end make sense, because all the prophecies have come to pass, but after that, there is eternity and all things are made new. This is where the hope comes from.

At the beginning of John's Revelation of Jesus Christ, he is writing a letter to seven churches, explaining to each one what it needs to do in order to be ready for the end. Repent and be saved, or if you are not lacking, beware, because the enemy if God is out to get you if he can. The whole book is a warning that time is running out and the devil is running to and fro on the earth to see who he may devour. Emperor worship is the prominent way to go in this day and age and the Caesar's are very happy about it.

The rapture of the church comes. This is when Jesus takes his own up through the clouds to be with him while the world goes through the great tribulation. If you have seen the movie or read the book called,

Left Behind, you understand this idea. There are many opinions on this subject also. There is Pre Trib, Mid Trib, Partial Trib, and Post Trib. I adhere to the Pre Trip position; the rapture comes first. The reason I do, is because I take the Bible literally. God said it. I believe it. That settles it. There are two groups concerned in this issue; Israel and the church. The day of the Lord has been promised Israel by the prophets of old. The marriage supper of the lamb has been promised to his church. The bride is the church and the groom is the Lord. The marriage takes place in heaven. They return to earth to have a wedding feast with those who survive the wrath of God on all the nations.

The tribulation is the time of trouble for Israel and the whole world without God. When the church is gone, so is the Holy Spirit, who keeps the peace. The enemies of God are in charge. This is also a testing of those who claimed God and went to church, but never gave their heart to it. There will be a remnant that will find faith and live to see the return of Christ, but they will suffer until it is over.

The church will be judged for their rewards (crowns) and some will be disappointed, because they did not go all the way with God. When those years are passed, there will be the Millennium kingdom, where Christ will reign for a thousand years of peace. Satan will be bound in a bottomless pit. A new heaven and a new earth will be born. All the covenants will be fulfilled and all the prophecies. The dead in Christ shall rise and all the saints of old will come for their rewards.

There is a Heaven. There is a hell. Trust in the savior, and all will be well.

BIBLIOGRAPHY

NIV Study Bible, Zondervan, 1984

The New Unger's Bible dictionary, Moody press, 1977

Strongest, NIV, Exhaustive Concordance, Zondervan 1999

Israel Pocket library, History Until 1880, Keter books, Jerusalem, Israel 1973

Chronological and Background Charts of the Old Testament, Revised and Expanded Edition, John H. Walton, Zondervan 1994

Things to Come, J. Dwight Pentecost, Zondervan 1958

Printed in the United States
By Bookmasters